T0123245

THE HOUSE WHERE GOD LIVES

VERNELL EVERETT

authorHOUSE®

AuthorHouse™
1663 Liberty Drive
Bloomington, IN 47403
www.authorhouse.com
Phone: 1 (800) 839-8640

Published by AuthorHouse 09/21/2018

ISBN: 978-1-5462-6142-1 (sc)
ISBN: 978-1-5462-6141-4 (e)

Print information available on the last page.

Scripture taken from The Holy Bible, King James Version. Public Domain

WHERE MY
GOD LIVES

CONTENTS

CHAPTER ONE
THE BEGINNING

he Smiths felt blessed to have a healthy baby boy. The celebration lasted far into the morning. It had been a long night due to the long laboring time. But, the midwife was the best anybody could remember. She could count the babies that were lost under her delivering on one finger. They were blessed to have such a God-fearing midwife helping their womenfolks to bring new life into the community.

The women were the main participates in the birthing of a new member to the human race there in the back woods of Mississippi. The men could hardly remember at what time the new-comer arrived. This was nearly always true if the new member took its time coming out of the womb. Slow birthing gave the men time to consume a good size jug of smooth drinking whiskey and a glass or two of home-brewed sipping wine. Nobody had ever heard the men complaining about the long hours they had to wait to welcome their blessings. The men thought delivering babies was the women's job, with the help of the Lord, of course.

The big over-sized baby boy arrived just before noon on one of the rainiest days of the year. The wind was making such a fuss until the baby's daddy and uncles could not hear the screaming and rejoicing from the house. They were too far into their celebrating to care much about what the women were doing. The men knew the situation was in the hands of God and mothers. The men main jobs were to come later, until then their job was to stay out of things that they didn't understand, like mothering.

"Hey y'all! Why ain't you drunks in the house helping with the newcomer?"

"Grab you a snort and tell us what in hell is going on, brother-in-law!"

"Am I to believe that you two Smiths don't know what time it is?"

"What in the world are you talking about, brother-in-law? It's eleven thirty right now and this watch is right on the nose."

"Oh Lord! These fools don't know that the little fellow has been here so long he is nearly old enough to get a job."

"What did you say!"

"I said that your son is nearly an hour old. You nuts didn't hear the whooping and hollering going on a while ago?"

"See you men in a minute. Save me some of my own brew."

Smith wobbled to the house to welcome his son into the world of men. It was good that the newcomer was not old enough to recognize his drunk daddy the first time they met. Sam's buttons on his shirt nearly popped off when he touched his son's hand.

"Get back and don't touch the baby before you wash your hands. There is no telling where your hands have been at, or on."

Sam didn't have time to wash his hands and rock the baby. That was women's work. He had to get back to his celebrating with his brother and brother-in-law. Sam had to go down to the pub and see if there were others that he could brag to. This was what he had been praying for every since he and Mae had been married.

"Come on you buddies of mine. Y'all can't look down on me now. I'm the daddy of a fine boy. Garth said he has to be the biggest baby that she ever had the pleasure of bring into the world."

"You are acting like the bigger the baby is at birth, the

prouder you should be. Do any of us whiskey-sipping daddies ever tried to see this big-baby thing from the mothers' side?"

"Oh, hush yo mouth and come on. The drinks are on me today."

"Let's git 'em while the getting is good. We might have to wait until he has another nine-pound baby boy before we git this chance again."

"I'm ready. He is your brother-in-law."

"Yeah, and you are the baby's uncle the same as I am."

"You men try to come up with a proper name for this great man of tomorrow. I'm open for suggestions."

"I got it! After all, we do expect my little nephew to grow into becoming a great leader. The greatest leader the world ever had was Abraham. That's what our pastor said."

"Man you are pretty smart for a brother-in-law. Let's drink to that."

"The young man will need a lot of input from men like his uncles here. We can't put much trust in your contributions. You have some serious mental limits."

An assignment was given the new-comer even before the baby had an official name. The young men fathering the new generation had high hopes that they were fathering an army of men who would do what their daddies didn't have the guts to do. Voting rights, equal rights, and just plan old rights were beginning to penetrate the thick skulls of the black, and some of the white, men. The pressures were on for some kinds of change in the way the citizens thought of themselves. The little newcomer would have his work cut out for his daily life.

"Hey honey! How is my little man coming along?"

"Don't you come in here smelling like a beer hall. Get yourself in there and wash up before you come near my little angel."

"Okay, okay! I just want to make sure that all was okay with the big fellow."

"Everything is okay, no thanks to you lush heads."

"Thanks a batch, Garth. We couldn't have done it without you."

"Bye, Mr. Smith. Go on and do like our newest mother told you."

The new daddy went back to the people who he could relate to; his drinking partners. The wind picked up and threatened to bring some heavy rains. This kind of weather in the northern part of Mississippi was the norm for late summer. These locals welcomed the rains on one hand and hated it on the other hand. They got together and thanked the gods for the rains but felt a deep guilt for sitting around sipping rot-gut while God was at work. The guilt didn't last no longer than it took for these goof-offs to get to their hefty supply of soul lifting beverages.

The baby had to be made ready for the preacher's blessings the first of the month. These three weeks would be plenty of time to get the little guy ready for the public's eye. The fussing mothers and grandmothers had to start making baby cloths. They had no time to get a head start on this mission because they didn't know what the new-comer was going to be. Rainy weather was the perfect kind of weather to get together and make a big fuss over the work that only women had the skills to do. The grandmothers were the main players in these kinds of big doings.

Grand babies were the steps the young women used to become grown and respected members of the church and the community. Mothers didn't let their daughters grow up until there were grand children to boss around. In rural Mississippi women had to be one kind of mother or another in order to have a respected group to belong to. After a woman got to be in the great grandmother category she usually became one of the mothers of the church.

"Don't worry 'bout booties for this little rascal. I have some that my Joel never wore. It looked like my sisters thought booties were all their little nephew wore."

"That's right Edna. Your family bought, or made your little Joel enough cloths for five babies. But, look how many there is of y'all. It's hard to believe that a small man like your daddy had that many babies in him."

"Daddy was not the one having us. That skinny man was always off somewhere drunk or working. There were times when I don't think he knew us at all. He paid us very little attention unless we got in his way."

"When is the big day for this little handsome bugger?"

The first Sunday of next month. I think he might just be walking by that time."

"Don't rush him, Mae. You'll be sorry when that time do come. Right now you know where this little fellow is at all times. You wait until he is crawling and walking about and see how hard it is to control the future king's whereabouts. He'll be into everything he can reach."

"You are right. I can well remember when my little cousin was sitting in the yard eating chicken mess. His big sister was suppose to be watching him at all times. Mary had her mind on other things other than watching her little brother's every move. You know how she was."

"How she was? Edna! How she was? She is still as man-crazy as she has always been.'

"Show you are right. She has gotten worst in her middle age. That old girl has trained more young men than Uncle Sam has."

"Mary's biggest problem was her shape. She had the shape that caught every man's eye from a mile away. She knew how to switch her rear end too."

"I think we will have enough baby cloths to last this little bugger forever. That is if he didn't grow none."

"That's what we were talking about earlier. This little Mr. Smith will grow faster than Johnson grass. That's why we don't need more than a few changes for the little scamp."

"Yeah, Edna. Remember when your little bad boy was so small until we could hold him in the palm of our hands. How much did he weigh at birth?"

"He was premature. You would never think for a minute that he weighed only four pounds at his birth. Judging by the pain I was having, one would have thought he was half grown'"

"Your mother and our midwife show had their hands full with your whooping and hollering all night. You were groaning and moaning like he was big as a horse."

"Oh, shut up Mae. You should have heard yourself. Good grief, what carrying on you did. You even cussed out the baby's daddy. I started to spank you myself."

The godmothers, along with the natural mother, were ready to show off to the next pastor of their church. Yep, they had the answer to a lot of their questions relating to man's sinning and going to hell.

The first Sunday was as perfect of a day as a good dues-paying church-goer could expect. These loyal servants of something beyond their understanding, took the perfect day to be a sign from on high.

After the pastor did his thing, the women had their closeup looks at the baby from head to foot. They checked the size of the poor guy's feet. The sisters were of the opinion that a less than perfect baby was the sign of sin, or something that was within their control. That is, control of one's sinning. The big sin was not being true to one man. Very few could past the test of being a one-man's woman which put the majority at risk of having a defective son or daughter. But the worst bad luck was when an in-between child was born. This was a child who was born with two different souls. One who could not make up his/her mind to which gender to belonged to. Of course this would come into play down the road. The daddy and his celebrating biddies decided to call the great man of the future, Buck.

Abraham, or Buck, grew like a weed for the next four years. He kept a keen eye on his little sister Linda too. Linda came along less than two years after Buck. But, Buck was the man of the house. Buck's daddy planned to make Buck into the man that no other member of the family had ever been. He wanted Buck to be a new creation of his daddy. Sam wanted a son who might be the kind of family member who would make his people self-respecting. Self-respecting colored men were seldom to be in this part of the great state of Mississippi. The kind of men who Sam meant by self-respecting was the men who could and would stand their grounds no matter what. This was the kind of man Sam Smith had always wanted to be but didn't have the courage to do what it would have required in his day. He thought that the time had come when this standing up for one's self and his could be practiced without costing lives.

"Mae. I wonder which college this big man will want to attend and what he will want to be. We will have to start planning for the day when we will have to make a decision."

"Don't you think you are a bit ahead of things? My god, the boy is only four years old!"

"It's never too early to start training the next great Frederick Douglass. This boy is a born champion. We all will be proud of him one of these days."

"You mean you will be proud of him. You should be more worried about him being proud of you?"

"Hey, watch what you say now. You were once proud of me, or were you?"

"Not too much. I married you because you were all that was remaining after all these pretty girls got their picks. You were a left-over."

"My boy is gonna make up for all that I missed. He is gonna make his daddy a happy man. You are the one who better get your act together."

"Tell me something Mr. big man. Were you ever proud of your daddy? Can you give an honest answer to that question? I know I never were too proud of mine."

"Yeah! Most of the time that is. He was a mighty man around the house and when he was sober. He did make us shame of him at times. But, he had his reasons for getting drunk and making a fool of himself."

"It's hard to find people our age who looked up to their parents. I don't know a one who wanted to be like their daddies and mamas. Don't that make you wonder?"

"The only man in my family who everybody looked up to was, you know who that was without me telling you."

"He was that old crazy great uncle of your. Uncle Benny. Man, he was as nutty as a fruit cake. I remember the time when his brother and your grand mama had to hid the nut in the potato bank to keep the law from shooting him. I remember my mama and daddy kept us indoors for days. They didn't dare leave the house either. There were crazy white folks all over the place looking for any excuse to beat the daylights out of some colored people."

"I know he was our hero for years and would be today if he was still alive. He just might be. Some say he died in prison up north somewhere. We never got the body, or any other proof that this was true."

"Colored men like he was couldn't last too long here in this country. There is not much here for them to do and be themselves. You remember my grand uncle was a chip off the same old tree as your uncle was. He had sense enough to get as far north as he could go here in the United States. He went to Maine. He was half white anyway. Up there in that cold weather he blended right in with the rest of the citizens. He even married a white woman."

"He had children too, so is the rumor. He did bring one or two home when he came to his mother's funeral. His wife never came though."

"No she didn't. He knew better than to come strutting through our county with a white wife on his arm. I said he was a bad apple, I didn't say he was stone crazy."

The winds of change were beginning to blow through the southern communities. Changes to what? That was a hard question to answer. There were no examples to use as role models or maps showing the directions to what or how. The roads that would lead to the utopia the people were dreaming of had not been surveyed yet because nobody knew which direction was the way.

"Don't forget that school starts at nine o'clock am. I thought about taking the day off but Mondays are when all hands are needed on the job. I didn't become the top hand by missing Mondays."

"You got that right. You didn't miss a day when these children were born. The last time you missed a day was to go to your daddy's funeral and that was a Saturday. You would not have missed that day if your boss had not insisted."

"Aw, come on Mae. I'm not that bad. I will take off on special occasions and you know it. Remember the time you had pneumonia? I babysat you until you were on your feet."

"You did that alright but you used part of your vacation for the time you took. You used a week of your two-week vacation time."

Little Bro. was growing like a fattening pig. The boy could eat all day and half the night. The boy had the kind of personality that made people cater to his constant whining.

"You are gonna have to get into your son's rear end sooner or later. I dropped by the school today and was told that this here son of yours had won all the other boys marbles and before giving them a chance to win them back, he used them to bird hunt. Can you imagine that?"

"It's not his fault that the other little scamps can't shoot marbles. Let the boy be good at whatever he decides to do. Do you want him to be no better than the others of his company?"

"That's not what I'm talking about and you know it. Take a few hours and watch what and how your son do things. He thinks that he has to be the best there is at what he do. Is that the way a young boy his age should think? He is just eight years old."

"What am I suppose to make him do?"

"I just want you to start paying more attention to what your son is becoming."

"I'm paying more attention than you may think. Am I to tell the boy not to do his best just because his best offends or takes away from his fellow playmates?"

"I'm just saying that the way he is he'll have no friends. The teacher says that the other little boys have stopped playing with your son. What do you think that spells?"

"That tells me that he is following his own mind, whatever that is. We will have to be awful careful how we encourage, or discourage the boy. Do we want him to be like we are, or have always been? Huh?"

"I don't want to discourage the young man either, but I do want him to fit in somewhere. He is gonna have to get along with these boys."

"You know honey, I have always regretted the way I was brought up. We were told what not to do more than we were told what to do. Look at our generations of Blacks and tell me what you see. How many became what you would consider a success? Why did they fail to blossom? What stood in the way of them being more than poor old colored folks?"

"There were more than one or two things standing in our way. It was us most of the time."

"That's right. It was the older generations that were blocking the road to a better way of dealing with what was. I have no plans to stand in the way of my son or daughter while they are deciding to be more than we will ever dream of being."

"I know what you are saying, but let's don't forget who we are while we push our young men to out do the generations that came before them. They will still have to find their places among us. We are all they have."

"I know what you are getting at. His generation will have a high price to pay for the kind of possibilities we are asking them to make possible for those who are to come behind them. It is very little they can do for us. The best we can do for our sons and daughters is to move out of their way and provide the support they will need."

"I have to agree with what you are saying that we all will have to do. It still scares me out of my wits just thinking about the problems that these young folks will have to face. You know these folks ain't going to give up any of their advantages without a fight."

"If there is any people in the world who know this better than we do, I would like to meet them. There is one thing that is as clear as the nose on our faces, we do have to get prepared to pay the price to be men and women in our own rights. We will have to depend on each other rather than depending on something outside our own control"

The two dreamers sat and thought for a while before getting back to the daily pressures of just hanging on for dear life. They were good citizens of the world that they knew.

CHAPTER TWO

BUD

"Buck, when are you gonna open that jar of peaches?"

"As soon as you leave and go home."

"Is that any way to treat your best cousin? If it was me I would give you over half of them old peaches. They just might be sour anyway."

Bud was a year younger than Buck, but a few pounds heavier. Bud was Buck's sidekick. Where Buck went, Bud went. What Buck got into, Bud got into. After all they were first cousins. The cousins were celebrating their sixteenth and seventeenth birthdays.

"Come on now, open them there old sour peaches. There is no telling how long they have been in that jar."

"OK! Grab yourself a spoon and a cup."

"That's the cousin I know who is talking now."

"I didn't tell you to get a bowl. I said for you to grab a cup, a tea cup."

"Alright you two in there. I'm trying to hear my stories. You boys don't be so loud in there."

"Buck don't want to give me half of that jar of peaches you gave us. Lord have mercy on him."

"Don't bring the Lord into your cheating and eating habits."

The two eating machines were like cows. they could eat all day long without taking a break. They were growing like sprouts in a field. Bud was at his cousin's for breakfast and for the rest of the day during the spring breaks and summers.

The two were in the sane class in school too. Buck was the one who did both their homework. They were straight 'A' student. Bud was a bit slow when it came to doing his own homework. He totally depended on Buck to get the tough jobs done such as doing night work and homework.

Both Bud's parents worked full-time jobs and was usually in town shopping the days they weren't on the job. Bud's folks left the boy on his own most of the time. They kind of depended on their kinfolk to look after the boy. This lack of attention by his parents left Bud free to do as little of toilsome work as he could get away with.

"We got a test coming up Monday, Bud. Don't you think you had aught to poke your head in that math book once in a while?"

"I am, I am. I don't have to know too much as long as my smart cousin knows. You study the math and I'll study the English. How do that strike you?"

"Maybe you need to sat next to Ida Mae. You and her are kind of stuck on each other, plus she is pretty good at math."

"NO! Do you think I want Ida Mae to know just how dumb I am in math? No way! I want her to believe that my high grade come from me."

"Don't you fool yourself. Them girls ain't fools. They know what they see everyday. If she didn't know, Rachel will tell her. Remember who they are, boy. Them two gals belong to us and they tell each other everything. They might not talk about their private doing as much as we do, but they sure have a lot to giggle 'bout."

"Do you think they tell all what they do? I'm talking about the really personal things that we do?"

"Don't we tell each other about all? If we do, you can be assured they do too. Them gals be holding their breaths together ever month waiting to see if their periods come on. Don't you know anything boy? Bud, how much thinking do you do about what you and Mae will do if she got in family way?"

"I try to think as little as I can about that. Even Ida Mae won't talk about such. I know one thing her daddy would have a fit. Mr. Washham ain't too friendly to me as it is. If his little girl got in family way I might have to catch that bus that left here last year."

"Rachel and I try to be as careful as we possibly can without having to stop seeing each other at all. It's almost impossible to keep my hands to myself when I'm near my beauty."

"What would you do if she did get knocked up?"

"I think I would have a bigger problem with my mama and daddy than I would with Mr. and Mrs. Turner. I can hear Daddy now, 'You fool. Didn't you have sense enough to protect yourself? Now what you plan to do with the rest of your life?' He would go on and on. You know Daddy has already got me through college and into some high government position."

"I believe your old man would have a nervous breakdown if you spoiled his dreams of you making him into a hero. He is always bragging about your high grades and on and on. What would your mama say?"

"She would have to save me from my daddy. Mama don't push me like Daddy do. She often tells him to let me be a boy before being a man. But he insists that what I do today will determine my future, and his of course."

"I've even heard your mama tell your daddy to let you be a boy. I heard her say to him one day, 'Buck is a boy so let him be a boy.'"

"Rachel and I are thinking about just playing it cool from now on. We sure don't want to ruin our lives before we have a life. Rachel is planning on going to college the same as I am. Don't Ada Mae have her eyes set on becoming a teacher?"

"She sure do. That's about all she talks about when we are

by ourselves. She wants to teach kindergarten children. She loves children. I guess she had to because she has babysit her little brothers and sisters every since they came into this world. Her mama would be back at work within a few weeks after the little ones got here. Then it would be up to the children grandma and Ada."

"Rachel wants to be a secretary at a hospital or in city government. She thinks that those jobs will be wide open for women of color by the time she gets ready to go to work."

"I wonder if our girls ever think about how their husbands might feel about some of the decisions they have made. Their husbands will have a say in this. What is your thinking on working wives, being that your mama has never work outside her house?"

"I haven't thought too much about that. Mama has always been right there in the kitchen when we needed food cooked. I can't really imagine how a house without a woman in it at all times would be like. I have been at your house a few times when your mother was at work and it was different. Your little sister and brother were at it all the time."

"Then you wonder why I'm over here all the time. Your house is always smelling like good eating. Your mama keeps the kitchen heated up all the time. That's the kind of kitchen children want. It is depressing to go into a cold and unfriendly kitchen looking for something to put in your belly. I started coming over here as soon as my little brothers and sister got big enough to stay home by themselves. or Grandma had them."

The time seemed to drag by the closer it got to spring break. School was not the favorite place to be for young men who would rather be fishing, hunting or working for a few dollars to spend on their girlfriends. Buck had learned to drive by hanging around his uncle Joe. He could hardly wait until his eighteenth birthday so he could get his driving license. His daddy was not in a big hurry for Buck to get too involved in making money, driving automobiles and chasing girls.

"Buck! I want to see you and Bud spending a little more of y'all time hitting them there books. You will have to start thinking about college. You have one more year and 'bang' there it is. So, you know what you will have to do to get prepared for that time. You will have to start right now. What about Bud? What is he thinking about his future?"

"Bud don't talk much about going to school after high school. He thinks a high school diploma is enough for anybody. I think the same way at times."

"He is right if things don't change. But, believe me, it will come a day when we colored folks will be able to write our own tickets to where we want to go and how we are to be treated. Yes sir, I can see the handwriting on the wall. I want you to be ready for those days."

Buck never argued with his daddy when it came to schooling and talking about future opportunities for colored folks. He felt like banking on such future opportunities might be risky, but what did he have to lose. The worst that could be, he would be an educated colored cotton picker. He hadn't planed to work for any of the local Whites anyway. He and Bud had been thinking about big city life where one could get lost and never be heard from again, that is if need be.

"Everybody close your books and get ready for a test. We will see if you students have been paying attention. This is checkup time. Buck, would you come up here and get the test papers?"

"Yes ma'am."

It was so quit in the classroom until a mouse peeing on cotton could be heard. It was easy to tell the ones who knew their stuff by the expressions on their faces. Buck had no problems with home work and passing the simple test. His hobby was reading and his text books were nearly the only books he had to read. He and a few others were confident in their abilities to ace the simple test.

Buck was almost as informed about history and literature as

the teachers were. The teachers in Mississippi were famous for being the most uneducated teachers in the world, baring none. The schools and teachers that taught there were as close to being illiterate as Buck's daddy was. This bunch could hardly recognize their own names if they weren't printed in large capital letters.

"Buck! What have I told you about messing with the girls when they are trying to think? Do you want me to flunk you because of the way you act in class?"

"No ma'am! I was only telling her that her dollar was hanging out of her pocket."

"Young man you better mind your own business and finish your test."

"I'm finished ma'am."

"Then I suggest you be excused until the others finish their test. Did you hear me Buck?"

"Yes. I heard you. I can hear real good."

"Sometimes I wonder if you can hear at all. Show me your backside as you go through the door Drop your test papers here on my desk on your way out. Let's go!"

Buck had time on his hands. He had it rough trying to find something to do with the hours he had left after surpassing his nearest challenger. The grown folks didn't always find his styles of having fun to their liking.

"Let's go hunting tomorrow afternoon if the weather holds. The squirrels should be jumping bout now. Them things will be gathering nuts and building their nests before cold weather sets in."

"Sounds good to me. Mama will welcome some fresh meat for the table. She can take one little skinny squirrel and feed the whole county and make it taste like there is meat in them dumplings."

"My grandma is the one who pushes me to hunt. She even buys the shells, as you know. Do you have any twenty-two cartridges?"

"Not many. I might have three or four, but you have enough for both of us."

Buck's grandma loved her some wild meat. She came from a time when wild game was the only fresh meat the family had. She often told stories of her father's methods of taking the stink out of skunks and making the meat eatable and tasty."

"I don't think I could deal with a polecat no matter how you fix him. Just knowing what it was would make me throw up. Good god!"

"You have to remember Bud when that was. We are talking about fifty years or more in the past. We black folks would eat anything in those days. We pretty much will eat anything now. You eat hog guts don't you?"

"Yeah, but they are clean. But. I see what you mean. We eat according to what there is to eat. I have heard that a human being will eat another human being before he starves to death."

"Bud! If you had read your literature books you would have read that. I forgot that you can't read."

"I don't have to as long as I've got you around. You read and think enough for the two of us. We both don't have to spend both of our lives with our heads stuck in a literature book. Don't you agree?"

"Heck no, and you know it. If I was of the mind that you, and most of our kinfolk, I would not have my nose in a book half the time. I would be doing like you which is chasing these gals when my main girl ain't watching. Why are you scared that you might have flunked this test we just took?"

"That is your fault. If you hadn't started acting like a fool in class I could have copied more of your answers. No, you had to start acting up so you would get thrown out of class. I know what you were doing."

"Aw come on Bud. You know I wouldn't do that to my closest cousin. You and me are like twins."

"Aw shut up. I'll get you for this down the road somewhere.

I've got a job helping my daddy on the weekends. I will be rolling in hard cash in a few days. Let me see what you do in class then."

The boys rushed home to get their rifles and hit the woods before the old folks could find chores for them to do, which there was never a shortage of.

"Let's go down in the bottom pasture and check out them red oaks. There is lots of acorns on them so I hear. Old T.J. has been hunting in the area and where that trifling old man hunts, there is bound to be plenty squirrels."

T.J. was one colored who the young boys thought was one bad cowboy. T.J. did very little work for the powerful people whether they were black or white. The Coloreds were the only people who did get a little out of him. There was one thing about the man, he could do just about anything a home needed done, or an automobile. But, the part of him that got the attention and admiration of the young black men was how he treated white folk. He had no love for them at all.

T.J. had spent years away from home but nobody really knew for sure where he was all them years. Some said that he was up north living with his aunt waiting for the Whites, who he had taken the liberty of kicking the mess out of, to die. A few said that the man was in prison those missing years. But, he was the hero of the young **wannabes**.

"Howdy Mr. T.J.! How are you this evening?"

"I'm doing 'bout as good as a man like me can do. What are you two buggers doing over here this time of the week?"

"Buck thought up this hunting thing when we left school this afternoon. I just as soon be over to his house eating my aunt's cooking as to be standing here fanning flies."

"I know what you mean. She can put together a mess of mean dishes. I love them teacakes of hers. She nearly always saves me some if she can hid them from you greedy rascals."

"Have you seen any squirrels running around here lately?"

"If I was you I would mosey over into them hickory trees.

You will find a few that came in to take the place of the batch I slaughtered Monday. I'm just out here today enjoying this great fall day. I wouldn't shoot a squirrel if it jumped on my head. Mama would have a fit if I brought more wild meat home for her to clean and put up."

"We'll get them buggers, Mr. T.J. Let's git Bud."

"Good luck boys, and be careful!"

The great hunters were glad that they didn't have to worry about T.J. being out there hunting in his area. Nobody who they knew of took chances of annoying the adult bully. The strange thing about the supposed-to-be bully was he was about the nicest man over forty in the community. He was forever ready to lend a Colored a helping hand.

"T.J.'s presents in these woods makes me feel safe as a baby in his mother's arms. You know what they say about him popping up at any time and anywhere in these woods, don't you?"

"The man saved a boy's life a long time ago. Daddy said that Mr. T.J. just happened to be in the woods hunting as he usually did when he happened upon a lynching."

"Everybody knows what happened after that. The crazy colored man did something that had never been done to the ruling class by a poor darkie."

"We know the story of how he got his start of rambling the woods day and night. For days after that both Blacks and Whites were scared to leave their homes for fear of meeting up with a bunch of angry fools. The Whites were looking for any reason to harm a Black to teach all a object lesson."

"We have been able to travel these here back woods and pastures without having to worry about some crank pots every since. Thanks to our crazy Negro."

"Here we are! I think I see one from here."

"You go around to the other side and I'll cover this side."

"Oh no you don't. You go around to the other side and I'll stand here and wait for them little jokers to run to my side of the tree. Bud, did you believe I would fall for one of my own tricks? Remember who taught you that trick? Boy, you are getting dumber by the minute."

"Okay! You are a better shot than me anyway. At least you think you are."

"Watch out for them piles of cow messes. You know how you curse and carry on when you step in a fresh pile of cow droppings."

"You aught to hear yourself sometimes when you slip on chicken do do."

"Hush boy and go on to the other side of the tree if you want a good meal of fresh squirrel meat for tomorrow's supper."

The boys had found a tree full of good eating. They managed to bring down three of the fattest gnawing animal they had ever seen. Their jobs were not done with the killing of the little rodents. They had to clean their kill. The women didn't jump to clean the boys kill as quick as they did to clean the daddies' kills. Getting the sisters to do the dirty work was out of the question. The boys could get killed by making such an outrageous suggestion.

Bud knew better than to take such dirty work to his house. His folk didn't have time for such work. They didn't mind sharing a meal of wild rodents once in a while as long as they only took part in the consumption of the meat.

"Gosh, you feel this cold wind? It sure looks like we are in for a bad winter. It's getting cold much too soon."

"When are we gonna start hauling our kindling wood?'

"Weren't you paying any attention where you were putting your big feet? We have walked over enough good kindling to last a life time. Boy, I don't know what we gonna do with you. We will start hauling some of this fat pine kindling as soon as we get the pickup."

"Are we gonna sell some like we did last year?"

"You bet your dumb butt we are. But, we won't over do it like we did last year. We were the first of the homes that ran out and had to brave them cold northern winds looking for more kindling."

"I tried to warn you but you are one hard headed cousin. You got too greedy to listen to your old dumb cousin here. We paid for your mistake too."

"You spent as much of the money as I did, but you will never let me forget. You were right in there eating hamburgers and sitting your butt in the movies the same as I was. Your gal enjoyed the cash flow too."

CHAPTER THREE

THE END OF BOYHOOD

Mr. Smith was getting worse the more he went to the doctor. There was only one doctor in the county seat and he was not too concerned about the health of the colored population. Mr. Smith would be instructed to take the pills given him and get plenty of rest. There was no known ailment to address. It was not old age because Sam Smith was just getting into his fifties.

"The old doctor is getting slower and slower, Daddy. We had to wait half the morning and he had no other patients. I can't make sense out of the way these old geezers think and do."

"I know you have always had problems understanding how these folks of ours act. Look at it from the other side. Now put yourself in their shoes. If you came from the same background as they did, don't you think you would be about the same as they are? I know what you are feeling because I've felt that way all my life. The time is near when things will change."

"I know. That's is what you've told me since time began. There has to be something that we can do to help bring change now. Look at you. You need all the care that we have right now. If you don't get the doctoring you need it will be too late soon."

"Let's go son. He said he had not eaten his lunch and he took a break while he had no customers."

"Did you ask him what did he think we were."

"Do you think it would have done us, or him, any good?"

"Yes, it would have done me some good and it wouldn't have mattered what his answer would have been. At least he would have had to think something about it."

"I know what I have taught you. Some of the thing I have insisted you do I was not ready to do myself. But, I wanted to prepare you for the day when you would be in a position to succeed at what you decided to become. It was downright dangerous for my generation to jump in the face of these folks and demand to be treated the same as the Whites were treated. What do you say about that?"

"I'm just tired of sucking the hind tit and saying nothing. I would feel much more like a man by raising a little hell even if it did get me in a little trouble with them jokers. We have nothing much to lose. They might be dumb enough to think we like being treated this way. You heard what our old outlaw Negro did the other day?"

"You mean that crackpot T.J.? That man has always been a little on the other side of having good sense. You see he never married or had children. What kind of rewards do he get for being a sassy old man?"

"That's the one. He didn't back down not one inch. He stood his grounds without blinking an eye. Me and Bud was standing almost as close as I am standing to you. Mr. Wilson acted like he wanted to belt Mr. T.J. But he thought better of it."

"Only a man like T.J. could hope to get away with doing such. You see he has nothing to lose but an empty life anyway. He has nobody who would be left out in the cold if the unthinkable did happened to him."

"Sometimes I doubt that is the way it is with the man. Judging from the way he looked, he was totally pleased with what he did. I have never seen a poor man stand as tall and proud as he did when Mr. Wilson was dumbfounded and had to tuck his tail and run. Me and Bud felt part of the pride surrounding our hero. Mr. T.J. was the tallest man we had ever seen. There was nothing we wouldn't have done at that moment to be in that man's skin."

The young men all over the county were talking about what their larger-than-life T.J. had done right on the front street there at the county seat. One would have thought that Christ had returned to the earth to save all lost souls. The young children could be heard shouting saying such as, "I'm gonna T.J. you one if you don't get out of my way."

"How you feeling Mama?"

"I'm feeling pretty good, thank God. I might not be once I hear what that old prejudice doctor had to say. Did you ask him what I told you to, Buck?"

"Yes Mama. He gave me the same old worn-out answer. He said that Daddy needed to get plenty of rest and don't worry too much about his condition."

"That's what I thought he would say. He wants us to worry about as much as he do, and that ain't none. I'm going to ask you and Daddy to think about going down to your uncle's in Mobile and seeing a doctor."

"I have told Daddy the same thing. You heard us the other day when he could barely get out of bed. This just ain't right for a man no older than Daddy. He will not even eat like he wants to get well."

Mobile was not the nearest big city where there was more advanced medical practicing going on, but they had kin folks there. Mobile was not a distant that could not be driven round-trip in a day. It was less than one hundred miles away.

"We will send Uncle Moses a wire telling him what to look for and when we will be arriving. He might have his phone back in and we can call him. Let's plan on going down the first of next week. Bud and I will have our pay for the logs we cut this week."

"Thanks son. Now I feel better. Maybe we can get some answers that makes sense even to us dumb old country folks. I know we must appear dumb as door knobs to these big shots, but we have lives of value too."

"This is exactly what I'm telling Daddy. We might aught to change how we treat the man instead of waiting until he changes how he treats us. After all we have the most to gain. The man has the most to lose if you ask me. He won't be jumping at the bits to give up what he thinks is his due. I believe that we will have to make the demands and back them up before we will be respected enough to be heard."

"I admire you for the way you think, but you will have to play the game with a few things in mind, What and who are you putting at risk,"

"That's what Bud, Fred and I have been discussing for days. Neither of us is thinking about getting married and having a family to raise under these social conditions, therefore we are in a perfect position to take chances that could create a better community for our kind."

Monday came almost too quickly. Buck, Bud and Fred made ready to get Mr. Smith to a doctor that old Uncle Mosses had already. He was to see the specialist that was his brother's family physician. They decided to use Fred's daddy's Ford sedan. The short ride was about two hour long. This was because Fred didn't dare get a ticket which was an easy thing to do in their world. Four black men riding on the US highways on Monday mornings would have to be law-abiding good driving motorists to avoid getting negative attention from some highway patrolman who was out to get some pats on the back from his superiors.

"Slow down boy! Don't you see what's over behind them trees."

"I see him and I bet the bastard is asleep and don't have a clue who we are. He is too far away to recognize us as being Colored."

"You might have something there. Fred, you look like one of

them from that far off. Fred sat closer to the window and raise up high so he will see your light color."

"Aw shut yo mouth. You ain't too much darker than I am."

"Will you guys listen to this bull? If I didn't know better I could easily mistake this boy for a country red neck."

The doctor was a mild mannered older white man who took his dear good old time and gave Mr. Smith a good going over. The doctor might have been taking his good old time because he usually didn't have too many patients on Mondays."

"Mr. Smith, I will study these finding and check the x-rays and have answers to your questions in a couple of days. How do that sound to you?"

"Thanks a lot doctor. How much do we owe you?"

"See my secretary. She will take care of you. You might pay it all, or half now and the rest at a later day."

"Thanks again doctor. My daddy will feel better now, I hope."

"Let's keep our fingers crossed and pray for the best. Good day men and drive carefully."

"We'll see you the next time big brother. Thanks for letting us use your doctor for your brother instead of us having to search for one. I feel better already."

"Tell the women we send our prayers. Tell them we are still going to church every chance we get, and for them to make sure that their men do the same."

The next few days seemed like an eternity for the Smiths. The old man had gotten so quite until he had to be dragged into the family conversations. Mama could be seen gazing at her one and only life lover with a frown on her face.

Daddy, what do you think about us starting a small protest about us having to sit upstairs at the movies when we are paying the same price as the Whites?"

"Ask yourself, is sitting with the Whites worth the price that you all might have to pay? Sometimes we pay far too much for nothing."

"No Daddy, that is not the point. We were trying to start where if we do lose we won't go hungry. We have nothing to lose if they shut us out for a while, or until their wallets start hurting."

"You boys be careful how you talk to these old crackers. They won't take it lightly when it comes to letting their girls sit among black boys. That will be the stumbling block at the movies. Y'all might be better off starting your protest where there aren't any females close by. Somewhere like a men shoe store."

"I called Uncle Mosses this morning and he said that the doctor had the report. He is mailing it to us, but he wants to talk to me and your daddy together. He don't want us to misunderstand some of the medical terms used."

"Mama why don't we drive back down there tomorrow and see the man. I want to hear every word he has to say. It won't take us but half a day to do the round trip."

"You might have a point. I'll get your daddy ready to wake up and listen."

They rode in silence most of the way to Mobile, Alabama.

They all were of one mine, anticipating what was to be. Buck was beginning to see changes coming across the hills like a mid-summer thunderstorm. They were at the doctor's office at opening time. They were brought right in and the doctor got right to the point.

"I'm glad you came back because I would like to take a few more x-rays. But, I see there is a small tumor on you lungs. Now don't panic because we do have a serious problem but I think it can be treated successfully. Do you hear me?"

"Go on doctor. Daddy is quite when he expects serious news."

"I will check out the best treatments, that is in my opinions, after I get the results of the next set of x-rays. Okay?"

The crew felt better knowing that there were new treatments for these kinds of tumors. The old doctor assured them that the end of the world was not yet. They had time on their hands. He had explained to them how the new methods for treating these kinds of tumors worked. He said that from what he could see the tumor was local.

"We will have to plan at least two trips a week for your treatments, Daddy."

"Let's see if we can schedule the trips around your college classes. You are doing too good in college to let a thing like what I got derail you. Do you understand?"

"Show I do. If we can't make your appointments flexible, I can change my college class schedules. I don't think scheduling classes and doctor appointments will be the big problem. Getting you back in good health is. I can always go back to school."

"The other thing we will have to deal with is the money and time spent traveling to and from. I know gas ain't much of a problem, but what about Fred's car?"

"I have that all worked out. You just leave that to me. I agreed to lend him a hand with his field work one day a week in exchange for his time and vehicle. How do you like them apples?"

"I know you try to be a smart butt at times. But, your solution to this thing do make some sense. I just don't want you to get the big head on us. You are starting to act like you are the daddy and I'm the boy."

"That should make you feel good. You have raised a son who is willing to take over at times when it is needed. Ain't that's what raising children to be responsible adults is all about?"

"I guess you and Bud will be in charge one of these days which makes times like this a good time to train for it. The two of you lending Fred a helping hand more than pays for the use of his car and his time. That boy works like the work is gonna bite him. I can't stand to watch that young man trying to hoe a row of beans."

"What service he gives us is an example of how everybody can be good to his fellow man only if the opportunity comes shuffling by."

The traveling back and forth won't be too bad as long as the weather is pretty good. There comes times when Mississippi's weather can turn deadly and cause wrecks on the narrow highways. Half the drivers on the road are not professionals. They have driven more miles in the fields than they have driven on the roads.

Buck and bud were kept pretty busy with the added chores and the tramping up and down the road to Mobile. They had a second choice to the transportation problem, that is if it came to be too much traveling to do daily. Daddy had a choice of staying with his brother during the treatment times or continue doing what he was doing.

CHAPTER FOUR

THE VALUE OF STUPIDITY

"**B**uck, I think you better let me and Fred handle this deal. We can get more money than you can."

"It's almost unbelievable how that works with these people. You two make me shame to be Colored at times. But as you say, what you two nit wits do and how y'all act is what works."

"You went to school too long. Your schooling has a negative value when it comes to dealing with these good-old-boys. You see we have never had to deal with a smart butt Negro before in these parts. At least the Whites didn't have to be bothered with a smarty Black. The only smart Blacks were our preachers and school teachers."

"You can do good business with our people if you could forget that little education and do business as usual with our good old white folks. Now you just stand back and watch us do business with Mr. Orange. You could learn something about how to get along here in your neck of the woods."

"I know what you dingbats gonna do. Where do you think I've been all these years?"

"Yeah, we know. You spend a lot of time learning what a smart Negro don't have any use for and that's good white-folk's sense. You just remain in the truck so you can pull up to wherever Mr. Orange points to. We gonna show you how good black-folk's sense works miracles"

"Moning Mista Onge! We gots ya a fine load hea. Jess you set yo eyes on dem cross ties."

"Pull over here and unload them onto this here pile and then come in the office for y'all money. You hear boy?"

"Yesuh, we hea ya. Give us a minute or two. We don wanna wast yo time."

"Take a count of that Mr. sporty man. Do you think for a minute you could have gotten the top dollar for this load by using that uppity-Negro jargon?? Not in a million years."

"It's a crying shame when a man breaks his rump for years learning skills he ain't allowed to use in his community because of ignorance and absurdity. What in the world has man come to?"

"Buck! don't forget who you are talking to now. These folks didn't become what they are within the last year. No, they have always been this way. You are the one who told us this wisdom. Remember you telling us how it once was illegal and a big social NO NO for a Negro to learn to read? Remember?"

"Yeah, I know, but the more I think about what and who we and our folks are and how they treat each other, the madder I get. I remember reading somewhere where the writer said that this country had the potential of becoming a much greater country if it would use the skills of all its people. We Colored people ain't allowed to use what we have learned. We have to play the roll of fools so that we don't offend some dumb illiterate Black or White."

"Folks do say that your little education went to your head and you act more White than is becoming for a Colored. Your acting so high up and all, makes other Blacks brand you with thinking you are more than we are. I'm just telling you what some of your own kin say about you."

"I better not hear one say something like that. I would have a mouth full to say to him or her."

"Don't make promises that you can't keep boy. You don't know who is saying these things about you. Bud and I know that education didn't do all they are saying it did to you. We know you were a snooty little rat long before you read your first book."

"Uncle was the blame for part of your high-stepping attitude. He use to tell you how special you were which got on my nerves like crazy."

"Why did it piss you off? Why did his bragging about his only son make you so upset? It didn't stop you from coming over eating everything you could get your hands on."

"Ah Buck, you don't know much to be so smart. Bud didn't have a daddy there to make him feel special like yours was doing to you. Good gracious, don't you know anything?"

"I fail to see how we need to act like cultural fools just to get along in our own country. I won't let some butt hole make me become my own worse enemy."

"I believe most Blacks would ask the same kinds of questions, but they have nobody to address the questions to. So, you are the one who has all this book learning so where do we start harassing these local white boys?"

"Let's start with the lumber yard. We'll try our plans out on old man Orange again. The next time we are there I'll do the wheeling and dealing. How do that jack your breeches up?"

"This coming Saturday will be the beginning of a brand new Buck, Bud and Fred logging crew."

The men went home to practice how to act like they were sophisticated. They didn't have to be too high up to be above the average White or Black upper class in their community.

"Well Buck, did you and bud get some big words down in them thick heads of y'all's. What is this I hear you men planning to do?"

"Daddy, we are tired of letting these half-baked folks force us to be crazier than they are. The average one of these uppity folks don't have sense enough to pour water out of a boot. We know this. They, with our cooperation, are causing all of us to be as nutty as a mad dog."

I've been waiting for you three to come up with something like this. I'll tell you men what I will do for your project. I will get the lodge brother together and see what we can do to back you boys. They won't get directly involved, but might be some help if you three get your necks in a noose."

"Thanks old man. You might be needed with this educated son of yours in action. You see what you were asking for when you were praying for an intelligent boy? You see how this kind of thinking in the heads of Coloreds can backfire."

"We are all God's creations and its best that we remember that. We are all part of the total and share an equal chunk of the guilt."

"We are off to start a new variety of God's creations. We will teach the other side what you have taught us. The high class boys are the ones who seem to forget what you just said."

The three hotheads were riding high on winds kicked up by their important mission. They could hardly wait until they got to the lumber yard and old man Orange.

"Here he comes slower than ever. He is never in a hurry to wait on us. Let's see how this works. Don't you two say a word. Act like you can't hear, see or talk."

"Well! What have you boys got here?"

The three men sat as if they heard nothing.

"Are you boys done up and gone crazy or something?"

Still not an eye was blinked. The boys mumbled something to each other that Mr. Orange didn't hear. Mr. Orange cocked his head in their direction so he could use his good ear to pick up on what was being mumbled.

"Well if this don't be all. These Blacks have up and become completely unhinged."

"Oh, were you speaking to us, Mr. Orange?"

"You damn better know I was. What in hell has gotten into you nappy headed fools?"

"We didn't see you walk up. I told my cousin here that I thought I heard something. Would you repeat the question that you asked, Mr. Orange?"

"What has gotten into you boys?"

"What boys are you referring to Mr Orange?"

"You and them two who are with you."

"Oh, you are calling us boys. Okay, we have a few ties here for you. These are perfect which you can see for yourself if you can see at all."

"Stack them where you usually stack them."

"You mean stack them in the high-price stack where we usually stack them. Will do, Mr. Orange."

"I believe you made a mistake with your figuring here, Mr. Orange. These ties are exactly the same as the ones we always bring to you. Can't you see that?"

"Are you calling my calculation wrong? Are you out of your right mind?"

"What do you men think Bud? Are these the best ties that we have cut this year and I mean baring none."

"You are right Mr. Abraham. We done a very good job hewing these cross ties. Yes sir Mr. Abraham."

"Those are my figures and that's that. You can take them or leave them."

"Mr. Orange, we will take your figuring this time simply because we have unloaded them grade "A" ties. The next time we come here with something for you to buy we won't unload it until after we agree on a price. You see we have a say in how much we sell for more than you do. After all' the choice is ours. Do you understand what I'm telling you, Mr. Orange? Or should I put it another way?"

"Let's go Mr. Abraham before Mr. Orange have a heart attack. You see how white he has turned?"

"The poor soul is still standing in his office door staring at the rear end of our truck. Buck, you will have to go a bit easier on these high-class citizens of ours."

The three men rode toward home wrapped in a cloud of glory of which neither had ever experienced since they had stopped believing in Santa Claus. The few dollars that this heavenly feeling had cost them was nothing compared to what these men shared while dealing with the big boy. These colored men would have something invaluable to share for the rest of their lives. The black men had a better high on than they could have gotten from drinking a gallon of rot-gut.

"Well, how did you men come out in your dealing with Mr. Orange."

"Daddy, you and Mama should have been there and seen what we saw. I have never been made to feel so whole before in my life. For a while I thought the old red neck was gonna drop dead right there in front of us."

"Tell me about it."

"I questioned his figures and asked him to make sure he had it right. This was after we had sat there without getting out of the truck until he came up to the truck to see had we gone nuts. He had to come to us and demand us to answer his questions. We pretended that he was not talking to us and we didn't acknowledge his presents for a while. This really sent him out of his mind."

"Buck used his perfect English while trying to deal with the tie buyer. He responded by insisting that we accept the lowest price he had. We did because the satisfaction we got from watching him more than made up for the few dollars it cost us."

"I told him that his figures had to be wrong. I hesitated a while before I came right out and told him that he had made a mistake. This was after we thought we had accomplished enough and better get going while we still had our heads on our shoulders."

"That's when I told Buck to get us out of there. Boy, that was one eye-opening experience for one lifetime. Gosh, we wish y'all could have been there."

"Mama, you would have been proud of me if you had seen that. You know how you always warn us to be careful when dealing with these powerful men. But, I believe you would have agreed with us and thought it was worth the chance we took and the few pennies it cost us."

"I don't want you boys to bite off more than y'all can chew. These folks can do things to people that seem impossible for one man to do to another. Tell them about that Jones boy back in nineteen hundred and forty-six,"

"I still get chill bumps when I think about those days. You men have heard the story a dozen times. What your mama is trying to tell us is that the same could happen today. She thinks these folks haven't changed that much."

"This is the point that we are trying to make. We know they haven't changed their minds about who and what we are, but we have. We have changed our own minds about who and what we are. If we were them why would we change and short-change ourselves? No, we are the new men in the woods."

Before the month was out the news about what these black unorthodox idiots were doing was discussed at every colored dinner table in the community. The young boys were getting a big charge out of hearing their mamas and daddies talk about the steel nerves of their three heroes.

"You two know what we have done, don't ya? We might not be welcome back on Mr. Orange's lumber yard again. If not, what do you men suggest be our next move?"

"You know Buckatunna ain't much further away than the distance we are driving now"

"We'll have to wait and see if the old man survives our last meeting and see where we all will be better off by treating each other with a bit more respect when it come to being fair and just.

It is a crying shame that a people have to be stone idiots in order to remind his fellow citizens that they want to be treated like human beings."

The men continued to be the new men of the colored crowd. Their reputation of being proper and smart Negroes was spreading slowly into the homes of the white families too. They were often reminded of the old days when these kind of Coloreds were dealt with a lot more harshly. When these thoughts crossed their minds they would remember some tails of their local crazy man. T.J. was still used as a record breaker even after he had outgrown any need for such chance-taking.

"If old half blind T.J. took the chance to save as many of us from the man's noose as he did alone, we have it easy to do what we are doing. At least we ain't shooting people in the butts like he did. He got away with shooting a few nuts. You know we might be able to get away with what we are doing because of what our crazy old T.J. did."

"Yeah, if we can last without us having to get down to these men levels and become human monsters like they are. If we do have to slap a few heads, so what?

"Well, we might have to become a night-walker like T.J. became. But, we won't have to go that far I'm sure."

"I certainly hope we will have sense enough to avoid the extreme measures they used on us dummies. I want to settle down and get married and have a batch of little folks, who look like me, some day. My girl ain't gonna wait for the magic question forever."

"You know Fred what we have talked about in the past year. Do you really want to raise a family under the present white and black attitudes, or do what we can to make some changes before hand? I don't want to put my lady through what she would have to go through by having a husband, and father of her children, out here trying to teach a bunch of stubborn fellow citizens that we are due as much as they are of what this country has to offer its citizens."

"I know, but it still makes my guts turn over whenever we go into our thing with these people. I even get a lot of negative advice from the same people who we are trying to help."

"Hush up! Here comes that old crazy man- Mr. Big T.J. Let's see what he has to say about what we are doing.

"Good evening men! How is y'all's work going?"

"Is it safe to assume you are referring to what we are doing to these cousins of yours?"

"Don't act silly for me, Fred. You know doggone well what I'm talking about."

"We have to be careful who we trust now days. We have uncle toms everywhere we look. How do we know you ain't one?"

"Boy, don't you mistake me for one of your kin folk. Now, let's start over"

"You know you are responsible for most of this what we are doing to all our folks. Every time we play these games we first rehearse what you would do under the same circumstances. Right Fred, Bud?"

"You was the one who put these ideas in our heads all right. Our folks blame you for what we are doing too. If these nuts get mad enough to try some kick back we are gonna point them in your direction. They will be foolish enough to believe us too. They know we would never have sense enough to think of this kind of stuff on our own."

"That's right Buck."

"Okay, cut the bull, now how is it going.?"

"You know Mr. T. we had never got close enough inside these folks' minds to realize just how stupid they are. I'm talking about more than the Whites too."

"I thought y'all would be learning some hard-to-believe truths. Your biggest problems will be a lack of support from your own. Why do you think I have always been thought of as being nuttier than a fruit cake?"

"We are getting somewhere in spite of what some think. Plus, we are beginning to have big fun. We can hardly wait until we have a chance to practice our preaching. We have never had it so good."

"What about you Bud? You ain't saying too much."

"He is telling you the truth. I once thought I was dumb, but, I'm a genius compared to what these dumb crackers and dumb Negroes have in their heads. Nobody tells the truth, not even to themselves. I don't know about us, or the god that created us."

"Man, I lost my faith in a just god a long time ago. I'm talking about I lost faith in the one they taught us about. If you don't believe in their religions, you are considered crazy as a road lizard."

"We are sometimes told that we are as nutty as you are. You are the man who will have to give account of our silliness when you get to them there pearly gates."

"What do you boys really hope to gain by what you are doing? Now think about the question and your answer before you say anything. Think about what is important to you."

"I don't have to think about it. I have always felt angry when I see how my people are treated by people who are as irrational as a mad dog."

"Maybe if I tell you why I chose to live the life that I have, it will shine some light onto me and show y'all who your role model really is."

"It's about time we got it from the horse's mouth. Let's get on with it. We have about two weeks to listen to your story."

"It started when my daddy told me that I would never get anywhere in this world until I learn to operate by the rules. When I ask him what do one do when he don't like the rules. His answer was, you should either forget what you don't like and follow the rules as close as you can or suffer the consequences for bending the rules. I watched him and his generation but found nothing that they had that was worth giving up one's life for. Not by a long shot."

"So, you paid the price. Now here you are with nobody to carry your name into the generations ahead."

"Yes I do to. I've got you goofy rascals to carry on the job that I started. You boys said yourselves that people will give me credit for the social destruction that you three will cause if you continue what you are doing."

The old man never tired of being accused of corrupting the young with his madness. He once thought he had been short-changed when his life was without close loved ones. He had never had a meaningful loving relationship in which a man is willing and ready to give up all his dreams for. The members of his generation didn't show him much happiness for having made the choices that they had made. He had become one-of-a-kind which he knew he would be remembered for. He was glad that his contribution to change could be seen in the generation's attitude following behind him. He love the thoughts. He was becoming a hero through his life's journey.

CHAPTER FIVE
New Revelation

The dreamed-of-life that was chased by the citizens kept the human race populated. This dream of something that might never be was leaving these three social mavericks behind. They had decided to postpone marriage and tying themselves down to the usual jobs that were available for men of their kind. Once they got caught up in the strong winds of the changes they were trying to bring about, they had been committed. Their mission had become their destinies which they could not deny.

"Would you excuse us for a moment Mr. Smith?"

"No! I am waiting to be waited on. We were here long before them boys got here."

"Did you hear what that black boy called us?"

"We show did. He called us boys. What in hell is this world coming to when a Black can stand here in broad daylight and in plain sight of the whole town and call white men boys?"

"My grand daddy must be turning over in his grave about now. That old man knew a Black's place and did everything in his power to make sure they knew their place and stayed in it."

The white men spent a big chunk of their time trying to be

true to what once was and is no more. The three colored men kind of felt sorry for the loss generation of their cousins.

"Look you men, we are gonna have to stop being so hard on our leading citizens. What would happen to our country if they decided to up and go back to where they came from?"

"Oh lord, let's don't even think about that. If they did up and leave you guys would be running around here naked as jay birds in whistling time. Don't you and Fred forget where y'all came from."

"Will you listen to that running mouth, Fred? He sounds more and more White every day. We are gonna have to burn them books that he keeps reading. We got to save this boy."

"Fred you are awful quite today. I won't ask what's on your mind because you will have to have a mind to have something on it' So, I'll ask a different question. What do you want to tell Bud and me?"

"I've been thinking here lately."

"That's your trouble right there. Did you hear what our buddy said that he had been doing, Bud? He has been thinking here lately. Who in heck told him that he could think in the first place?"

"Don't act like you didn't know this boy before now. He has always been as empty headed as an empty snuff box. Have you ever seen a bug or ant making a home in an empty snuff box?"

"That's enough men. Get up off that boy. I don't see much sense in any of y'all's heads, if you want to know the truth."

"That's enough of that junk talking. Who wants some tea cakes? Maybe these teacakes will give y'all something else to chew on instead of each other."

"Mama knows how to shut up a loud mouth. She always has something to stuff in it. Thanks Mama!"

"Why do you think Bud hangs around here all the time? He ain't over here to help with your night work."

"Speak for yourself Fred. You have to walk miles to get here, but you are never late for a slice of Mama's chocolate cake."

Finding fault with each other was a safe way to kill some time. Putting each other down was a safe way to talk about something that would hurt too much if it was not joked about. All young men had a rough crossing when it was time to make the jump from boyhood to manhood. But it was especially hard for men of color. They had to jump into a no-mans land without a parachute.

"Buck! Now that you are finished with your schooling, what do you plan to do from here on out?"

"I've been thinking about hightailing it for parts of the country where I will be allowed to use all this book learning. How do that sound to y'all?"

"I'll let you answer his question Bud. After all, he can't hate you because you and him are closer kin than half brothers."

"I've told him what I think. Uncle and Aunt have also told him what he might run into out there in the big cold world alone. He might have to leave this earth in order to find what he is searching for."

"I'm gonna fool you old ignorant Negroes soon. You just watch me."

"We sure hope you a lot of good luck, you'll need it."

"Let's get back to something that is possible right here and now. Let's stop by Rays and try his fresh batch of brew."

"That's the first time you said anything that made sense all day, Buck. What do you say Fred?"

"You know me. I will never disagree with the two of you. I'm with you boys all the way on this one."

These three men had not gotten into soothing their disappointment and frustrations with fire water yet, but they were getting there. Ignorant juice was the most used medicine for severe depression and other mental problems. If a person learned how to run the stuff and pacify the law all at the same time there was no limits to where he could go as long as he didn't forget some basic trues.

"Hey! Go easy on that stuff man! You will turn out just like your old uncle if you don't be careful"

"What's better to turn out to be other than a stand-up drunk?"

"That boy show makes some easy-to-swallow stump juice. Jess wrap yo lips around that for a good swig of heaven."

"Look ova there behind the smokehouse and tell me what you see?"

"That's old T.J."

Let's see what he is up to."

"Good afternoon Mr. T.J.! How is the hammer hanging this afternoon?"

"About as low as it can get without falling off. It looks like you future drunks have found the temporary answers to y'all problems."

"We don't have any problems once we get our fill of this good stuff of Mr. Rays. Look how happy Fred and Bud look. Have you ever seen anybody looking happier than these two losers"

"You know me. I've hid in a bottle since the times before you men were thought about. That's why I said what I said about your temporary solutions to your conditions. You see drinking won't solve one problem but will add new problems."

"Here take a sip of this fresh stuff and maybe you will feel better. Come on and have a sip with us."

"No, thank you very much. I don't try to find the answers to my problems in a bottle. I learned better than that when I was young like you boys. If I had continued to try and drown my social problem in a bottle of soothing stump juice I would be long dead by now. No sirree, I will sat here and dream about what might have been."

"You ain't too old to make changes yet, Mr. T.J. It is never too late to be all you want to be."

"That sounds good only if it was true. There are things that it is always too late to become. You can be born at the wrong time, the wrong person, the wrong sex and on and on. The only way to deal with some situations is to make the best out of it, whatever that turns out to be."

"Do you think that you made the best that you could of your situation? You never married and had children and so on?"

"I certainly do. I'm speaking for myself now and, I am not trying to give y'all advice. I made up my mind that I could never go through what I saw my daddy go through once when we were at his boss's house. He tried to explain it to me, but I didn't buy it."

"What exactly were you wanting at that time back in the day?"

"I wanted to see my daddy in the same frame of mind as the little white children saw theirs. They were under the mindset that their daddies were gods. They thought that their fathers were great heroes. How could we see our fathers and other black men as our role models after watching how they gave up their manhood just to eat and sleep?"

"We believe we know exactly what you went through back when you were our age. We get a lot of that kind of treatment too, as you know. It must have been twice as bad back then. The old folks call you that crazy T.J. and once warned us to stay far away from you. Now we know why."

"They were giving you all good advice. To use me as a role model like a lot of you did, and are still doing, was not the way to stand a chance of making a success out of your being here."

"Thanks Mr. Bad Man. We won't try your way of straightening out our social mess. We got some plans that might work better than what you hand to use."

"I see what you men are doing and I'm proud of you. Keep on harassing the daylights out of these folks, both black folks and white folks. I here them saying that y'all better be careful."

"That old man should write his story. It would be good reading for us and the younger men and women who are still in school. They don't teach in school the lesions that he could share with us. I have never read in our history books about the kind of Negroes I would like my son to become."

"I don't think that old man ever went to school, or did he?"

"If he did he didn't stay in there long enough to learn common sense. My daddy said that he was always a blockhead. But, I hear he can read better than the one that did go through the schools of his day."

"I have learned a lot about education within the last several years. You two nitwits have been nutty enough to help us get a look behind the front the Whites and the Blacks show to the public. Have you two buddies of mine realize how stupid we all are here in this state?"

"I have got myself an education that we could never have learned in school. I had no idea that we were as dumb as we are. I wonder why others haven't learned what we have."

"Look Fred, they were not, and is not, today smart enough to by-pass what they are taught by the crazy folks who are doing the teaching."

"There is one fact that we are getting and that is, we are having a lot of fun at these craze folks' expense. I was always aware of some of our planned and practiced stupidities, but I didn't know that the others were doing the same thing."

"Hold up you two and watch this here. Howdy boss man! Hi is you doing this hea da?"

"Oh, hi Buck. I see you are doing good. How is your daddy doing since he had his treatments?"

"He is comin long fine. I tell him you asked bout his healt."

"Okay, boy. You be a good boy now."

Buck stood and waved the man on before he dared to move. The Blacks were expected to wait until the Whites call an end to any encounters between the races.

"Were you guys watching and listening? Can you believe he actually thought I could be that ignorant with a college education?

He knows that too and still bought into the line of bull I just fed him. Can you believe it?"

"His kind of thinking is what makes me glad that I'm not one of them. I once thought, the same as you men did, that it was a blessing from God to be White. I'm beginning to appreciate being me more and more as I learn who we are looking up to."

"You two should start going to church. I'm not talking about y'all going to the outside of the church building, but to go inside. I heard a great sermon Sunday while you two were out eating fish sandwiches and drinking cool ade."

"You do have a good idea Buck, but you always tell us all about the message between Sundays. We get the message from the one who we hope to make a man-of-the-cloth out of. You."

"I think it would be a good idea if we all went in and shared the messages and see if we heard the same messages. Do you mud heads get what I'm driving at?"

"Okay Bud, come dressed for church next Sunday. Make sure you have an extra fifty cents in your pockets for the collection plate too."

"You just worry about your fifty cents. I'm a church man anyway. I read the Bible pretty often too. How many times have you read the Bible in the last five years?"

"I'll be in the front row next Sunday. I don't want a seat on the train that you hypocrites will be on. No sir, I'm gonna catch that holy train."

"Buck, you and Fred are headed straight for them there hot coals. You two are gonna reap what you two have sown."

"Where do you think you'll be at, Bud?"

"I'll be up in the promised land eating honey and drinking sweet milk. I'll be enjoying what I have earned from putting up with people like y'all, all these years."

"Have you men heard the news about Rob and sally?"

"Don't keep us in suspense all day. You know darn well we

haven't heard whatever it is that you are so eager to tell us. Stop messing around and come on with it."

"Robert and Sal have decided to tie the knot. It's about time too. They have been necking all over the place every since Sally's daddy died. That boy almost moved in with the family. Sally's daddy didn't like the man none after he caught them in bed together. He came back home one day because he had forgot his lunch."

"Yea, yea, we know the story. Now, when are they tying the knot and why?"

"The why part is the news. We have always figured they would get hitched sooner or later. She is in family way."

"Oh shucks. I've got my fingers crossed tighter than dick's hat band. My future partner is a bit late this month. So, that's what she said."

Fred, what do your future look like to you? Mama and Daddy remind me and Bud constantly about ours."

"That is one reason I'm inside the church every Sunday. I know time is not waiting on anybody. You and Bud, and this includes me too, will have to decided if you gonna continue to play games or are we gonna get down to business about our futures."

"I asked Daddy the other day something along them lines. He suggested I talk this over with our pastor. Now how do I do that? What question can he answer about marriage other than what we all have already read for ourselves?"

"He sho did. I saw how Uncle looked over at Auntee when he answered the question with a question. I know there were times when Unk felt less than the man that he figured his loved one wanted to spend her only life with. You can see this kind of disappointments on the faces of most of the older people."

"Well, anyway, Rob said that he was planning on moving north where his cousins were. You know he has some education like you Buck. He thinks that his chances will be a lot better up there in the big city atmosphere."

"I know he ain't planning on taking a pregnant new wife along on a wild goose chase. Sally's mama won't stand for her only daughter getting lost in one of them big-city ghettos."

"That ain't the way I heard it. The mother is the one pushing the man to go ahead and get settled with a job and come back for both, mama and daughter. Rob said his mother-in-law to be has had her mind set on move out of this part of the south even before the death of Mr. Mack."

"This brings us back to our same old question. What are men like us to do in order to be men in the eyes of our women and children? We know the cost required to stand up to the bull that we have to deal with."

"This is the one reason why I'm getting inside the church, Fred. I want to find a way to be all that my god created me to be without stepping on the toes of his other creations. But, the question is, how to do that?"

There were unanswerable questions relative to how much should a man give of himself to make room in his life for others to be all that they can be? The men on both sides of the racial broader were hung up on the same peg. It was a kind of common belief that there was not enough dignity and self-respect to satisfy all, therefore some of God's creations would have to go without.

"How did you see into what our pastor said about loving all men as you love yourself? We have been listening to that verse since we can remember. But, he put it into a context that almost made some common sense."

"You did hear the part about if a man slaps the daylights out of you, you are to turn the other check with a forgiving smile on your face. I can kind of go along with being big on the forgiving end but that was asking a bit much. I will turn my other check and smile after I knock half his front teeth out of his mouth."

"You missed the point, Buck. The pastor added something else to that verse. He said that God would reward you for following the instructions of that verse. He said that our God would be the judge and do the punishing. This would save you from sinning by doing harm to your fellow man. You see, this obeying the commandments takes you off the hooks."

"I wanted to ask the holy one just how far, or how many times is this forgiving and turning the other check go on before we are forgiven for beating the stinking mess out the offender?"

"Buck, you have a piece to go yet before you get the message. We are all God's children and must behave accordingly."

"I agree with you. This behaving according to the golden rules apply to us all. This letting God take revenge might also be understood in terms of his using me to punish the offenders. I'll give God a hand with his creations by letting him use me to teach the bad boys the lessons that they need to make them into good god-fearing men."

"Why don't we present this question to your daddy and mama, and others to see how they see this. We could be missing the point completely. You heard what he said about wars and other kinds of bad things we do to each other that would never happen if we left the punishing up to God."

"I'm all ears on Sunday. I would appreciate answers to the worldly questions and problems. I can't see equality, respect and peace being possible the way man relates to his fellow man. Even husbands and wives don't follow them golden rules. Is that hard to believe, or what?"

The pastor was known for the good preaching he did. The man of the cloth was wanted all over the county. His members usually felt safe and clean after listening to one of his borrowed sermons. He didn't always write the messages but he sure could deliver them. The man had a great voice for singing too.

"It's 'bout time you men attended church every Sunday. I see y'all inside instead of hanging around outside watching the girls. I know there isn't any other places to be on Sunday but the church, so it's good to see your faces inside instead of seeing y'all through the windows. The little people can now pay more attention to what's going on inside instead of keeping their eyes pealed to the outside."

"Yes Mama. I'm beginning to get the messages too. If what the messages say is true a man would have to be a fool not to follow the scripture. A good Christian following the teachings of the word will have an easy life, plus he/she will have heaven waiting for them. You can't beat that. Sinners have to be fools to not see this good stuff."

CHAPTER SIX
Religious Journey

Mississippi's citizens were believed to be the most religious subjects in the United States. They were also thought to be the poorest and most illiterate people of the United States. The first belief these good old boys and gals would agree with, but the last two, they had problems with. It was true that these good folks had some strong beliefs about who was responsible for most of the world's problems, and it was not them.

"The pastor really laid it on them folks up north today. He said that the monies behind the corruptions moving into the great state of Mississippi came from the north. He said for us not to worry too much about it because the Lord truly had an eye on them and what they were doing."

"I guess God is part of the blame for the fancy cars and good cloths these folks manage to swindle out of us old honest southern people. He says that they get paid top dollar and do next to nothing for them big wads of cash. He and sally sure appear to be doing good even if they are getting it somewhat dishonestly."

"Look you two, wouldn't you like to have some of their kind of corruption? If not forever but for a few years before you get too old to enjoy it. You heard what the minister said about the Lord forgiving us seventy-seven times for any sin that we might commit by accident. We would never do wrong forever and on purpose"

"Buck, you act enough like them northern sinner already. Now you are beginning to sound like them. Don't you listen to our leaders with both ears?"

"I show do and I watch them with both eyes too. I see you leaning toward the truth about what these folks preach verse what they practice. Pick one who you think wouldn't change places with one of our returning rich home boys or girls. When one of them shinny cars drive into town with two people in it, it leaves so loaded until there is no room for luggage. You have seen this."

"Some of the big educated Whites and Blacks are predicting that all the young men and women of color will be gone from Mississippi within a few years. I heard Mr. Ramond talking to one of the Harrison brothers about how our workers, men and women, are packing what little belongings they have and leaving without any intentions of ever making Mississippi their home again."

"Fred, listen to what you are saying. Who is more responsible for these folks leaving? Us or them?"

"I think the culprit is them high-paying jobs up north and that easy work. They can't be running away from hunger or love ones."

"That's absolutely true Fred. What do you think Bert? You've been up north visiting your folk. What did you see that draws us away from all that we know to go hunting for a promised land?"

"I didn't see too much that they had that we don't have right here at home. I know one thing I was ready to comeback home before I got a good tour of their town."

"Why were you so ready to get your lard butt back home?"

"I looked into the eyes of just about everybody I met but nobody would give me a friendly stare back. Not even the Colored. The Whites pretended that you were nowhere in sight."

The old dumb country boys had a hard time wording what on earth would make them leave their friendly and loving home for a strange land filled with strange unfriendly people.

"You men better start reading the Holy Bible more. Better yet, go to church. The pastors will read the old testament to you and it might explain the reasons people go in search for a promised land."

"I heard the sermon a while back about the exodus of Moses. Now that man was on a mission for God. He led the children out of the land of bondage and to their promised land."

"Bert, how did our homeboys seemed to you to be getting by when you were up there?"

"Like I said, I could hardly wait for that bus to run so I could get on it. You men don't know what it feels like to blunder among strangers all day without meeting a single man or woman who you have seen before."

"Did you think that our home folks were happier for being there? Or were they just too sensitive to what the gossipers would make of their moving back where they belong?"

"That what you are saying was a big part of it, yes. The other part was that our home folks done gone and married into families that ain't from here. Many hooked up with other southerners but they were from other parts of the south."

"What is it that you think that we are searching for, Bert? That which is missing from our lives, if there is anything missing. We might have all that we need to make the best of what God intended us to have."

"See y'all the first of the week if I don't see you in church Sunday."

Buck headed home, along with his cousin who was like his under wear. They could smell them beans, okra and ham a mile away.

"Mama! Where is Daddy at?"

"Oh! He had another one of them attacks and decided to try to take a nap. He said he felt like crawling in bed and staying there until he felt like jumping off the porch."

"What do you think Bud? Do you think it's time to get the old man down to the doctor for another check up?"

"It can't hurt none. It is past his appointment time."

"Let's us plan to get him checked next week. How do you feel about that Mama?"

"Sounds like a good idea to me."

"You'll have to convince the hard headed husband of yours to go."

"I don't believe there will be a problem. He is feeling bad enough now to do whatever we ask him to. You just go ahead and make the appointment, Leave the rest to me."

"They are doing a lot of roadwork on this old highway now days. Have y'all ever thought about trying to get hired on at one of these construction companies?"

"You remember us talking about this the last time we drove down here? You remember Bud?"

"I show do. You were the one with the good car. We would have to drive nearly a hundred miles a day most of the time."

The doctor took his good old time as usual to serve the colored patients, But he finally called his colored patient from far away. It didn't take long this time for the doctor to come up with what was the problem.

"Let's all have a seat men. I think you should be sitting down when I tell you what I believe is going on here."

"Come on and sat down Buck! You need to hear this more than the rest of us, except your mama and daddy."

"The cancer is back, This is my opinion. Based on what I can feel and see, we will have to go in and see what the total picture comes out to be. Now, I suggest y'all go home and talk this over and call me as soon as y'all get your heads together. He will have to be hospitalized here where I will be able to keep an eye on him. So, I'll wait to hear from you Miss, before I schedule the surgery."

"Doctor, what do you think our chances are for a full recovery?"

"Well, Mr Smith, I think we have a better than average chance of coming out of this in pretty good shape. Y'all pray and keep your fingers crossed. Okay?"

"Thanks Doctor."

"You are more than welcome Mr. and Miss Smith. I'll be waiting to hear from y'all soon. The sooner the better."

Hardly did anybody talk on the way back home. The little talking that was done was to Uncle. They wanted to get him ready to provide room and food for a few of his relative. Everybody had heard the doctor's report and believed that all had to prepare to be in the city for a while. The old man would not be ready to take the long ride every other day to see the doctor, or visit the hospital.

The following few days were lived in denial and knee jerking hope for the best. The pastor and the deacon board were called on to lend their prayers and voices to the list of request directed to the higher powers that be. The church had several prayer nights to address the Smith's health problems.

The family was encouraged to not wast too much time hoping for that miracle they all were praying for to come galloping through the door. They did believe in the power of faith and prayers but they also believed that God worked in mysterious ways too. The prayers were appearing to work.

"I see you slept right through the night. You must be feeling a lot better."

"Yes sir, I have felt none of the pain that I have been feeling. I'm beginning to feel like my old self. I might get to feeling like running a mile or two."

"I'm glad to see you are doing better, but you are still going back down to the city for that checkup."

"I knew you would say that. You bet I'm going back if for no other reason than to show old Doc that prayers might work better than his knives."

Buck and the crew put off taking the old man back for another week. It was hard for Buck and Bud to believe how much

Daddy Smith had improved. Buck was beginning to get really into this new power he was seeing the results of.

"Daddy, you know what I've been thinking here recently?"

"No we don't. Why don't you settle down here and tell us what it is on that unbalanced mind of yours. You have never had normal thoughts in your life."

"Look how much improvements you have made since we have been taking your case to the Lord. You said yourself that your pain have all but vanished. Didn't you say that?"

"Yes, because it's true. So, go on and tell us what do my pain have to do with what's on that peanut size brain of yours?"

"Stop making little of what Buck is trying to tell us. You know what you are saying is not nearly the truth. You have said from the time the boy was born that he was a special boy. Ain't that what you have always said?"

"Now let me finish what's on this pea-size brain of your son's. We know what the Bible says about God performing miracles through faith and prayers. Haven't y'all always believed that? Anyway, I have been having dreams that had those same effects from having faith in God. Maybe we have such a rough time in this here life simply because we don't have faith in the God that created us. How do that sound to you people's old ears?"

"We are aware of the powers of faith but we are not aware of what it do for the many who suppose to practice it. I was at church Sunday too. I heard what the minister was trying to say, and he is right up to a point. I know faith is working in my case and I can testify to the good it has done me."

"Do we need any more evidence to make us believe in the word? Some of us won't believe even though they are looking the evidence in the face. You heard him tell about Jesus's own disciples' lack of faith while standing next to him while he performed these miracles. Isn't that hard to believe that man has such doubts in the God that created him?"

"I have often wondered about that myself. I wondered how

were we suppose to have faith in something that happened two thousands years ago when the same people who wrote the histories had such a hard time believing and was eye witness to the miracles."

"Well, I can't explain how them folks could doubt the word of God. I'm talking about what we are witnessing right here under our own roof. I talked to Mr. Rush Sunday. Remember he had the same ailment you do and he never went under the knife either. That has been four or five years ago and you see he is still jumping up and down in the choir singing better and louder than he ever did."

"You know these doctors are more often wrong than they are right. This is more true when it comes to us than it is for the other side. Maybe we need to do our own treatments. We lost fewer people to these horrible ailments in my day than we do today. It's hard to know what is and what is not. It is a job for you young educated Coloreds to figure a way out of this racially discriminating system."

The old man got well enough to save the money it was costing them to go see fake doctors. Buck was beginning to get his program going by using his new found time. Bud continued to be Buck's right-hand man. Bud had no other place to be but over to his cousin's.

"Buck are you really sold on this program that you are determined to get going?'

Fred, how can you hear all these good things about what is possible and not try some of it? If you don't test what seems to be true you'll always have doubts. You will be forever wondering, what if."

"I agree with you but you can waste a lot of time trying to get milk out of a turnip root."

"I had a long discussion with our pastor and he seems to believe I might be the one called to save a few worthy souls. I have nothing much to lose here in these woods by trying any ideas I have. This is one of the ideas I have for my taking a trip up north, or to some other big city to see what they are teaching about the truth of the Holy Bible."

"Well you can travel in peace because you do have Bud here to look after your folks until you get this thing out of your blood, or in it."

"Fred, why don't you and I go together to Chicago for a couple of weeks. We can drive your nice car. People won't look at us as if we are just what we are; country boys and green as goose turds."

"I'll think about it. We better get on solid ground before we settle down to raise a family. Can't you see the hungriness in the eyes of the generations ahead of us? This feeling of regret is coming from them wishing that they had done something to make themselves proud before getting locked in to a system that's worst than being in jail."

"You bet I can see regret written all over their faces. Why do you think me and bud are still sitting and doing nearly nothing. We don't have to say much about it because there are no words that we know how to use that say what it is that we are missing. I have never heard it put in words before. The Bible comes closer to putting this monster into word than any other book that I've ever read."

What do you say about this little trip to explore the country side and see what we can find. We might decide to move north one of these days if it is as great as these hot shots coming back home say it is."

"Okay Buck. I'll give this crazy notion of yours some thought. See you in the morning."

The pioneers got their car ready for the long run. They even bought an extra spare tire. They loaded up with an extra quart of the best motor oil that money could by. Yep these two explorers were ready to ride into a new land of opportunities. There had to be a key somewhere to the doors of opportunity to becoming men in the Colored race. They won't leave a question that they can think of unasked. Yep, the hunters were on the trail with the scent of success in their noses.

"Y'all don't go up there acting like fools, now. Do y'all hear me?"

"Yes Mama."

The family stood and watched the two prospectors drive into the morning fog on their way to who knows where. The weather was getting a bit cool for the time of the year. The two seekers didn't want bad fall weather to catch them out of the south.

"Buck, you did mark the entire route on the maps didn't ya?"

"You just keep your eyes and mind on driving, I'll let you know when to slow down, speedup, turn and stop. You get me driver?"

"From what I've been told we better make sho we don't run low on gas. Some of these service stations are slow to sell to out-of-town Blacks driving through their towns. It must give their Coloreds itchy feet when they spot some of their kind headed for the promised lands."

"We know how to play with these white folk's minds. We did it too long to have forgotten it. They are about the same all over the world. You just let me do the talking, boy. You can pretend you are a deaf mute. That shouldn't be too hard for you to do"

"You just better keep your eyes on the maps and the roads. I've got my hands full watching out for the darn big trucks. Have you ever seen this many log and lumber trucks before? We must have passed a hundred truck hauling cotton and live stock."

"We should be pulling into St, Louis, Missouri before two this afternoon. After St, Louis it's only a hop and a skip to the windy city."

"You better not get too comfortable sitting there eating up our sandwiches and talking like I'm gonna do all the driving. You better get your lazy rump set to take the wheel once we get to St. Louis. Do you hear me, Mr map reader?"

"How in the world can I not hear you. You ain't tired yet and you are a young man. You should be able to drive at least two days before needing to rest. Now, drive on chauffeur."

"Oh my god, this boy has lost the little sense that he had,"

"At least I am an educated fool. That is why I can talk black better than any of you idiots can. I have learn how to sound black. That's why you better let me do the communicating with these great Americans."

The two lazy black men rode for hours without seeing many of their kind. The main highways did not usually run through the colored quarters. The railroads did, but not the main U. S. highways.

"There is a service station on the right on the other side of the coming up light. Now, you stay in the car and I'll do the buying."

"Moning Suh. We like to git some gas."

"How much you want, boy?"

"Kin we git de tank full. Boss man?"

"What part of Mississippi are you boys from?"

"We be fom de south end. Dat's nea de Alabama line. Suh."

"Where are you headed?"

"We agoing to Chacago. Dats a ways fom hea. We got a map but it be hard ta read."

"Let me see your map, boy. You got it upside down. Turn it this way, see?"

The station owner went way out of his way trying to help the poor Colored travelers. He even stopped his hired Negro grease monkey to lend a hand with checking the oil, tire pressures, radiator fluids and windshield wipers. Yep, the boys got class A services. Of course these nuts couldn't stop laughing for the next five miles.

"It will be a little late when we pull into the big city. I thought we might drive into the south side where our people are and take a nap in the car until morning. I told my cousin that we might do this."

"That's way tonight. I'm thinking about where are we gonna

get some good old home-fried chicken this evening. Them sandwiches were okay but they don't provide the same filling as chicken and rice."

"Like we were talking earlier, we will have to follow the railroad tracks to get into the Negro quarters. That is what I have read and heard from my cousins. The Whites don't allow the noise and smoke that is created by rail traffic to exist in their neighborhood. No sir, they don't want their families to be exposed to such."

"There you go again with that little book learning. You can glue your eyes to a roads that will lead us to our folks while your mouth runs on about how much you know about these highways."

"My rear end has never hurt like this in my life. Boy, you will have to get us a car with cushy seats instead of these wooden benches."

"Just listen to the college professor. He wants cushy for a butt that haven't felt anything cushier than a wooden bench since the last time he sat in his mama's lap."

"Why do you think we spend all our lives going to school? We do the things we do so we will be able to tell you servant class what you can do to make us more comfortable throughout our lives. What in the world do you think your job is? You even had the nerve to ask me to do some driving. You are lucky that I'm willing to read the map for you."

"Keep your eyes pealed for the side roads and the railroad tracks. We are near some city limits. I can smell burning coal."

"You are right. The town is about two miles ahead. We are near Lemay, Missouri. There is a good sizes colored population there. I believe I read where they build some kind of wagons there."

"Don't you miss the turn if you don't wanna walk. I'm hungry enough to eat flies."

""Do you see what I see?"

"I show do. He is turning down that dirt street just to the

right. Our people would be living outside the well-kept city. Slow down and I'll ask the young man where the colored restaurant is. There can be only one in a town this size."

"There he is"

Howdy young fellow. We are looking for a place to have a bowl of bean soup, or something. Can you tell us where we might get some?"

"Yes sir. You can see it from here on your right. It's called Aunt Sue's Place. You can't miss it. They have good pork chops too."

"Thanks a bunch fellow. Stop by and I'll buy you a coke, or something."

"I'll be there by the time y'all get there."

The restaurant was the typical joint for colored cafes. The restaurant was not short of customers. They weren't all paying customers but regulars. Flies usually don't pay for their grub. But, the cafe had just about any foods a hungry Negro could want.

"I haven't seen you two around here. Where are you handsome young men coming from, or going?"

"We are from the southern end of Mississippi. We are near Mobile Alabama. Most people have heard of Mobile."

"I have a relative living there. He is a second cousin of mine. Y'all gonna be here long?"

"Not this time. We just pulled in to grab a snack of your tasty vittles."

"Oh Lord, you'll have to excuse me. I was too glad to see some strangers come into our place here. There is our menu right on the wall behind your head Mr.?"

"I'm Buck and he is known by many names, but you might wanna call him by his Christian name. That name is Fred."

"Please to make y'all's acquaintance. I'll be back in a jiffy. There is today's special on your table. 'Be back in a minute."

"I believe I'll be happy staying right here if she is an example of what these ladies look like. Did you look into them brown eyes?"

"No I was busy fanning flies. Here comes our direction giver. What is your name young man?"

"My name is Little Billy. They call me Little Billy because my daddy is Big Billy."

"Are you ready to order?"

"This is the man who told us to come right on to your place for lunch. He can have a bite too if he wants one. Go ahead and tell her what you want Little Billy!"

"Don't worry about what little Billy wants. He is a regular and we know what's on his mind. Which ice cream do you want today, little man? Strawberry? This is your day for strawberry, ain't it?"

"Yes ma'am. I'll have three scoops if you don't mind."

"Three scoops of strawberry ice cream coming up. In the meantime y'all be ready to get some good service."

The men got their fill of the best chicken and dumplings they had ever had and this included Buck's mama's. Yep, they were wide awake and ready to burn some high test gasoline. The ten-year old automobile was running like a new car. It should because it had less than twenty thousands miles on it. There was no place to go in the southern part of Mississippi that made driving long distances necessary. The farthest the car had been driven was to Mobile once or twice a year. Other than taxing people to mobile or Laurel for medical reasons, the automobile remained in the barn.

CHAPTER SEVEN

The Big City

The giant city was as cold and indifferent to the separate demands of its citizen as a swamp is to its critters. The buzz and hustling was much too fast and impersonal for the boys to get their mind around. Nobody seems to have time to talk to them or to listen to them. They were total strangers to a world that recognized no individuals separately from all others.

The cousin was too busy to take the men around town on a sight seeing tour. The man was working long hours on two jobs and his wife was working a job and taking care of two children. There was no time to wast on visiting relatives.

"You know I would not be disappointed if you were to decide to get out of here a day early. I've had my fill of the big city for this time. Maybe if I had a long-hour hard-working job I wouldn't have time to care."

"Fred, I was thinking along them same lines. Let's git come daylight tomorrow. I'm sure my cousins will be relieved to see us out of here. I know they feel terrible for having to ignore us. Plus they don't really know me or you. We haven't seen each other for more than a few hours per year since I was born. We got what we came for anyway."

"What do you make of all the people who we have tried to know since we started on this trip?"

"Fred, you know how me and Bud have been trying to figure out where in hell do we fit into the human race. The more I think about this and try to find answers to our questions, the more crazy it gets.

I kind of knew that this country's people were pretty much screwed up all over, and it seems that I was right. What do you see wrong with us?"

"There is so many things wrong until I don't ask too many questions because I don't believe anybody have any idea of what the answers should be. I used to ask my daddy and mama all kinds of questions but I don't remember getting any answers. All I would get was advice about being a good boy and stay out of grown folk way."

"Men of our sort better get our stuff together soon or it will be too late for us to do anything. My daddy once thought that we were gonna see some changes, but I'm beginning to hear doubt in his voice now days. He says we ain't getting any changes because we haven't learned exactly what it is that we need to do, or exactly what changes that would be good for all. He says there is no admitted wrongs to address to get the ball rolling. He thinks that we tell so many lies to each other until we have no idea what the truth is, or could be."

"Is our problem that we have lived lives of lies so long until we have no idea what the truth is? You heard the sermon about 'know yea the truth and you shall be free.' Can we be so blind and scared until we will never know the truth?"

"You saw how people looked at us when we would try to start a conversation with them. They would grab their bags and hightail it for other places. They acted like they were afraid of something. Was it the truth that they are trying their best to avoid?"

"Fred! Did you see what was parked behind that old closed service station?"

"I saw him. I see him pulling into the highway."

"Just remember to talk the same talk that we use on our white boys and we will be just fine. Act as dumb and sub-human as possible and he just might buy our lunch."

"I remember your craziness when we were coming up here. I think I'll be able to handle the nut. It's still almost impossible to believe…. Ops, here he comes."

"Believe it and play the game."

"He is waiting for you to get out and come to him. Go on and remember what to do."

"Boy, you got a license to drive that car?"

"Ye suh, Mr. Police. I got it right cher. Gimme one minit. Hea it tis. You sho got good looking cotton up hea, boss. I bet I could pick a heap of dat stuff."

"We could use more good cotton pickers. Our Negroes done gone up north and got too uppity to pick cotton like they did when I was a boy. You look alright, boy. So you can go and get back to them fields in Mississippi. By the way why are you boys on the road this time of the week."

"We had a def in de family and we went to the funal. Boss. Dats what we doing on de road."

"Okay, get back on the highway and keep on through town."

"Thaka ya boss man. We wil do jes dat."

"It is still hard to accept how dumb these folks think we are. I felt like cussing that bastard out. Are you okay with the way these bozos think about us? I almost told that joker where he could poke his head. Yea, yeah, I know where that would have gotten us."

"I'm telling all that will listen that we will have to do the best with what we have, not with what we hope to have. I got some plans for the three of us when we get on our horses of righteousness again. We will ride hard too. This trip taught us that what we are seeking is not in Chicago. I can imagine that Chicago as being no different from the other promised lands."

The men rode in silence trying to find words that could be used to talk about what they had seen and make some kind of sense of it. They knew they would be asked to explain the results of their experiences on the U. S. highways leading to a dreamed-about world.

"Put your thinking cap on Fred because we will need something to say to our church members about what they can hope for when they decide to reach out for that missing blessing that they are praying so hard for. You want to know something Fred? I'm beginning to believe that the Whites are more cheated than we are. They are as miserable as our folks are down home."

"Do you think that might be one reason them people commit more suicides than we do. I have never heard of a Negro coming right out and hanging himself."

"Me neither. I often thought that may be due to the Negroes being too busy trying to please the man and his god to think about killing himself. I think we were of the mind that if we hung ourselves we would go to hell for destroying the properties of others."

"That is something to think about. We are religious from the bottom of our feet to the top of our heads. I wonder if that is good or bad. Maybe being head-over-heels in the church saved our lives. We gave ourselves to something we thought was bigger than we were."

"There is our service station. We might as well stop here where we have trained the owner to treat us like we are idiots. We won't have to break in another Wise White."

"Whatever you say boy. It's your time to buy."

"After noon b, uh, men. Filler up?"

"Yea suh. Kin we git a RC and some skins?"

"Hey boy, come and fill these men's gas tank up while they do a little shopping inside. Make sure you check the oil and water."

"Step right inside men. There is nobody ahead of you. Y'all have the whole place to yourselves."

"Do it strike you as being funny how nice the good white folks can treat us when they want our money and there is no other white folks around. You heard that rascal call us men?"

"Yep, I was looking right at him. He had a smile on his face too. I have a few ideas to share with our board of directors at church. Yes sir, this should be a great educational experience for us all. Our actions will have to be wrapped in a religious and brotherly loving blanket. Even we at our church wouldn't know how to start a social movement without taking the safe and holy route. We believe this is the safest route we have. These good old white Christians can become savages if they think they are being challenged outside of the church by a bunch of black rebels."

Buck concentrated at the summit of his limited mental powers trying to come up with a program that his people would buy into. He had to know what the other side would buy into too. There was one thing he had an advantage in and that was that his people knew the Whites much better than the Whites knew them. This gave the beginning of his movement a chance to succeed. The Blacks were willing to twist and bend more than the powerful Whites were.

"You have been scratching in that note book for days now. When are you gonna let good enough be good enough?"

"Daddy, I'm trying to get ready for Sunday. You know today is Friday and Sunday is first Sunday. Every ear will be cocked in me and Fred's direction. They think we have the answers to all their racial problems. That is those who think that there is a racial problem. We are trying to start on a journey that can cause a lot of trouble if it is not traveled carefully."

"We all know that. Me and your mama want this thing you have your mind set on to work nearly as much as you do. But we don't want you to wear yourself out even before you get the ball rolling. Most of what you are attempting will have to be done by ear. You are starting on a road with no signs showing which way is which."

"What is your take on this mission of your cousins, Bud?"

"I'm with him all the way. He will need all the help that the members of the church and his family can give him."

"What do you think about having a son in jail, or worse, Mama?"

"I believe we will have to think about more than our son. There are many many others who will be tied up with our son. He will have the mothers and daddies of others on his back too."

"The most dangerous people I will have to watch are the mad and crazy low class white religious fanatics and the Negroes who are getting rich off the way things are. These folks believe that if we blacks get the rights to vote and elect ourselves to high and powerful governmental positions the world would suddenly end in fire and brimstone."

"In some cases they might be right. We have the lowest educated bunch of all the groups living in these United States. We will have to put a lot more efforts into getting educated."

"Education will be one of the biggest projects that Blacks will have to solve for themselves. We don't need the Whites to educate us. We already have the means to learn to read and write. That's about all the average White can do. Our job will be to wake up our people to see the need to know more than how to read the Ten Commandments,"

"I show would like to live long enough to see the day when we become elected people who have the powers to take up our own crosses and march on to the top of Mount Calvary. I remember very clearly when I had the same ideas that Buck has. But, it was extremely dangerous to step on people social toes back in them days. Mama you remember your folks telling me to get my head out of my rear end and stay in a black boy's place."

"Yes I do remember the night that Daddy told you that. You show did what you were told. You black men have kept to your places forever."

"That's exactly what I'm trying to get us to see. We need to see the need for us to wake up and become the kind of men and women who have the respect of the world and especially the respect of our own. How is it possible for us to love one another when we don't respect one another and love who we are? We have to become beings who are worthy of their own love.:

"You got a point there son. I had never put it in them exact words but you are doing just fine. I'm sure the doors of the church will be wide open to hear what you have to say to its folks. Most are more ignorant about what you will be talking about than we are. We have been discussing this mess for a long time. I can tell you a few reasons why we dropped the ball."

"I want all the information that I can get. Soo, you got the floor. Bud! You and Fred get the junk off y'all minds and listen to a voice of one who has a questions to ask that have never been asked? Why didn't your gang chase after a better way of living?"

"Well, it was something that had no handles on it so we hand no way of getting hold of it. There were no college educated colored men in those days. We thought we had one of two choices to decide for making a life for ourselves. You see we had examples of a few who took the other road and ended up nothing. Our man T.J. is a fine example of one of us who refused to walk the straight and narrow. He might be a hero to some of you, but look where he is today."

"Go on Daddy."

"Bring me a glass of water. I haven't been this excited about what a few of us thought back in the old days in a long time."

"Y'all don't get him worked up too much. We know that his health ain't what we would like it to be."

"The chances were low to none that a maverick Black who broke the rules that controlled the relationship between the races were not doomed to a life of nothing. This was if he had a life at all. You know most men and women looked forward to having a family, taking care of their parents, grand parents and so on. Very seldom did we live long enough to see many grands and great grandchildren. This was especially true for the colored men.

Life was short already without us doing things to even shorten it further."

"That's at the heart of what I want to share with our church people. What do you think of starting this from the church and what chances do you think the church gives it?"

"I can't be too sure about which way the ball will roll. But, I do believe that whichever way you pitch the ball it will run into objections and blockage."

"I'll do some thinking on it tomorrow and dream about this tonight. Maybe the answers will come in the form of dreams. You know what the Bible says about dreams."

Buck spent the rest of the week asking questions and giving his side of what he thought should be. His girl listened quietly but withheld an opinion. She had gotten kind of used to Buck's dreams of becoming.

"You do know what our aims are, don't you?"

"I should by now. You had them same dreams of becoming first class back when we were in elementary school. Now here we are done finished college, got jobs, or at least I have, and you are still dreaming of being something that might be out of your reach."

"I figure we don't have much to lose and everything to gain by putting our best foot forward. If we don't we will be the spiting image of our folks when we are old and bitter. This standing up for what God intended for his children has to begin somewhere. I don't know of a better time than now. Bud and Fred both agree with me. Now I need your support."

"Well I've waited this long, a few more months can't hurt. I know if you don't get this out of your system you will be hard to live with. I won't have you blaming me for wrecking your dreams, not in a million years."

"I'm glad to hear you agree with me. Now let's get ourselves a hamburger before we head for your house. I want to tell your daddy what's up and get a feel for his opinion."

Sunday came before the great leader was ready. It would

not have mattered if the Sunday was three weeks away, it would have still been too soon. Buck's stomach would still be upset. He had been trying to have a bowel movement for several days with little success. He was afraid his efforts would pay off at the most inconvenient time in his life.

The full church on the first Sunday didn't help Buck calm his nerves any. He felt the eyes of every member gazing at him. He had to get over this stage fright if he was to do what his mission called him to do.

"Members, listen here for an important message for us to think about now and in the days ahead. The Lord has heard our prayers and figured it is time for him to act through his servants. He has chosen one of our very own deacons to carry out his plans for us. God want's your full attention for about thirty minutes. I'm sure you can do that for God and yourselves. Now here is Mr. Buck Smith."

"Good morning my fellow Christians. Phrase the Lord. I believe the Lord has given me a big job to do for our people and our country. I also believe that he intends for you to be a part of this important mission I'm assigned. Phase the lord.

I believe most of you know where another of your brothers in the Lord has been up to here lately. Would you stand up Brother Fred and let there be no mistake. Fred and I went to Chicago to prove, or disprove, these tales brought back by a few of our rambling kin folks and fellow citizens. We gathered as much information as time would allow. We can tell you one truth and that is we could hardly wait to get back home to you, our friends, and our relatives. We never felt as lonely as we did in the big city in all our born days. I had to hold Fred back from speeding. I had the help of the highway boys to lend me a hand with his eagerness to speed while trying to get out of the north.

I'll tell you something that we will never forget. That is how it feels to not see a friendly face for days, not one. The other part of this strange world, we didn't see anybody who we knew outside of my cousins. You talk about being in a strange world, that was it. We arrived at one thing for sure and that is if we want a better living condition for us and our women and children, we won't get it in the big city. We believe that we can have a better way of traveling through this life, BUT! And that's a giant but. The "BUT" what we are offering you is a chance to think seriously about is what we will have to do to change ourselves. We saw no signs of what we were searching for really existed this side of the big ditch. We think, that is Bud, Fred and I, that it is possible that we are the ones, with your help or course, who can bring changes for the better to our own lives. We have a plan that we will need a few brave and proud men and women to engage in. Now Listen to what we need to get started with.

We need about five or six volunteers to help us put together a plan of attack that will stand the best chances to succeed. Are you with me so far? If you have any questions just raise your hand. We will start a search for others across history who have done the same things that we are trying to do. This study and planning will take a while. But we can speed it up by meeting during the week and on Sundays after church. This meeting at church after the service will give the entire community a chance to ask questions and keep up with where we are at the time. We will give the community an update every Sunday until we are ready to start the actions. Are there any questions thus far?"

"What will be if the white folks get angry and decide to do what they have been known to do when something goes against their wishes?"

"I'm glad you asked that question, Mr, Johnson; This is the reason we have to make good solid and lawful plans to follow. We will try our upmost to stay within the law, but we will be treading close to the line. There will come times when we might have to react to law-breakers on the other side. I think we realize that risk. Yes, Mr. Ike?"

"This will require us hiring lawyers and other professionals to work with us."

"You are on the right track. Would you consider joining us, Ike?"

"You bet. I'm just wondering why it took us so long to realize what we would have to do. My son is into this kind of doing and he has been blabbing this stuff ever since he could talk. Now he will be coming out of law school with a big head. Maybe this will be a good and safe start for his civil rights law degree, what ever that means to black folks."

"Thank you Ike. Now lets get to these recruits we need to get up and going. We have one, Mr. Ike. Now who else can we depend on for fun raising, calling people, checking mailing lists etc. We will decide who will do what as the needs pop up. Take your time and give Fred the okay and he will record your names and be in contact with you. Thanks a bunch partners in promoting justice and may the Lord walk with us and bring along his blessings."

The first meeting showed these eager beavers some hope and promises. The community showed more interest than the ring leaders thought they would receive at their first meeting. The three community hot shots went home with their chests stuck out to the point of busting buttons off their church shirts and suit coats.

"Buck! Buck! I think we might be going in the right direction. What do you think, Fred?"

"I tell him all the time that he has the gift to talk people into going against their better judgment. His daddy has to shut him up at times when he gets going late at night."

"I forget you two have been sharing the same kitchen forever, and sometimes share the same bedroom."

"But, in spite of him talking us to death, he sure got the attention of the members of the community today."

"We got ourselves' a leader for this social equality thing. I hope he don't let this successful speech go to his head. You know how we are when we get a little social attention. This boy might have a future in the church."

"Alright you two, let's cut it out. Tell me what is your real opinions of how the members of the church took our mission."

"I did see a few frowns of confusion on a few old faces. I think this is to be expected. The frown were expressions of fear more than expressions of disbelief, I believe."

"I certainly hope so. To pull this off we will need all the help that we can get. We have a lot of the Whites who will be with us if we go about this with a high degree of understanding of both sides."

"Which Whites are you referring to?"

"Take a survey of who we will be dealing with. Let's us get to the roots of this thing we are attempting to do. Take tours and see what these people think they stand to lose and what they think they stand to gain from the changes we will be whooping and hollering for."

"It don't take a smart man to see that we have more poor and hungry Whites than we do hungry and poor Blacks. A high number of Blacks have always been better off than the average Whites."

"We will have to be clear in our own minds what it is that we are shooting for. Is it food, clothing, housing and so on? I don't think so. What would you tell our folk what it is that we are asking the other side for.?"

"How will we do what we have to do? What words can you use, Buck, to get the ideas across?"

"Let's talk about this beginning of the road that we are thinking about traveling on. Let's talk some about what it will be that each side fear. Once we get a handle on these fears we might be able to address the fears in a way that would put them to rest."

"What in the world do us Coloreds have to lose?"

"What about Mr. McDonald? Who is he in business with and who makes sure he has the support he needs to make money?

What about Mr. Melvin Turner who has it made working for that good old boss of his? People who are in these kinds of relationships will question any changes coming down the social highways."

"These are our own people who might get the wrong ideas about what it is that they have to gain or lose. Change is often resisted simply because of misunderstandings, or ignorance. Are we that far in the dark?"

"Listen up you two. Buck tell us what you have on your peewee mind that will help show a clearer picture of what it is we are supposed to be chasing. Let us hear what you have dreamed up in that big knotty head of yours. We know you have something even though it might be a head full of chicken muck."

"You two bone-heads give me the little minds that y'all got just for a minute. Y'all pretend that you are walking down the front street in town along sides of Billy Walker. All of you are the same age, the same size, dressed the same and have the same amount of money in y'all pockets. Now, this is the big thought you will have to understand. How is your situation different from his? Do you want to give your understanding of this, Fred?"

"I don't know exactly what the total difference between him and me is but I do know that I can't do what he can do. I can't go where he can go. Plus, I won't be treated like he will be treated."

"What about you Bud?"

"I wouldn't expect to be seen in the same way as he would be by neither people. You and I know better than to expect to be equal to him."

"You got it! Now go on and tell us why that is?"

"It's simple, even a nut would know that the Colored would not be treated like the White."

"Let me put this another way. What do one have that the other don't have? What allows this to be? What can be done to change this cockeyed relationship?"

"Buck, I would not have the same freedom as that white boy would have."

"Why not?"

"Because I'm Colored, That's the only difference that I can see. We Coloreds don't even expect to be equal to the others side."

"We are getting close to the answers. Tell me this. What do you think would take place if you tried to follow him in the front door of Hoppy's bar?"

"That question is easy to answer. Remember when T.J.tried that same thing?"

"Yes I do. That is the reason I'm bringing this one up. What happened to our old nutty social misfit?"

"He was arrested and thrown in jail. He was charged with trust passing on private property."

"Was he on private property? No he was on property that was licensed to serve the public. Was T.J. considered a member of the public that the lounge was licensed to serve?"

"Evidently not. The sheriff kept the dummy in the slammer for over a week because nobody would waste money on his bail."

"Let me explain what was, and still is here. T.J. or you, do not have equal protection under the law. You don't have the same rights as the other side do. Do you get where we will have to be careful at and point our efforts in a safe direction?"

"Yeah, Buck, we got it. Boy we will have to deal with the law before we can really get at the real changes here. The jails will be full of us colored nuts who are stupid enough to follow you with your hair-brain ideas. Do you hear the man Bud?"

"Yeah, I've heard him read this stuff from them magazines he picks up in town and through the mail. You should hear him and his daddy getting it on after supper some nights. We have a big job if we are successful at getting the law and the minds of the people changed. We might be the lambs that will have to be sacrificed to the devil to bring about these super changes in what is."

CHAPTER EIGHT
Contact with the Law

Mr. Smith(Buck) and his sidekicks started to spread their brand of social moral behavior every time the opportunity dropped in. These opportunities were dropping in every time they rubbed shoulders with the other side of the social highway.

"Y'all get ready to dance now because here comes our Pastor walking as if his god has just assigned him a mission. Get your best and proper self up front. We don't want to spoil the man-of-God's day."

"He sho is walking like he is afraid of being late for something"

"Morning Reverend! You look like you are on a special mission. What has you out and about this time of the morning?"

"I had a visit from our sheriff this morning early. He had a message for me to give to you three men. I thought I had better not wait not one minute."

"You just come on in here and have a seat. I think a swig of this good gut soothing medicine is what you need right now. Here take a big swig and give it a second to settle in them queasy guts of yours."

"Thanks a lot. Boy, I needed that like a drowning man need

rescuing. Yeah, like I was about to say, the man came all the way to my place to give me a message for you boys."

"I see you glancing at the jug here. Here take another good swig."

"That will do the trick. You men do know that Jesus turned water to wine for his disciples, don't y'all? Well, anyway, the man told me to tell you men not to be in town today carrying on with y'all mess. The Harris brothers and a few other white tramps will be waiting for y'all. He said that he would have no other choice but to lock you men up. He said that was the last thing he wanted to do. So, give me one more sip of that devil's juice and I'll get back to the church. You men know this is the day we clean the church from wall to wall."

"How do you feel now Reverend?"

"It is no wonder that we have so many members with a drinking problem. This devil juice can make a man stand up to just about anything. After a swig or two of that stuff, I feel like joining you men in town. I'll git now since I have done my job."

"Take it easy Reverend! Thanks for the warning."

"Well, it's about time the law got involved. I'm sure the newspaper will be on top of this too. This is what we have been waiting for. Now let's make some good-citizen plans."

"Hey! This pot of social soup is gonna start boiling soon. We better watch out or we will get scalded by the hot overflow."

"You men know good and well that we will not accomplish much unless the social pot of dissatisfaction boils over. This is a way to get the attention that we need in order to get the job done. Now, listen you two, we will have to be almost saints when we ignite our social time bomb. What is on that mind of yours Bud?"

"Y'all already know I'll go along with anything you two block heads start. If we don't keep on going we will have wasted a lot of time all these months of picking at these good old boys."

"Let's decide how far are we willing to go without giving these resisters reasons to go crazy. We want to look as if we won't bust a grape. We will have to avoid any physical threatening action at all cost. Once we show that we mean business without violence, we can do whatever is required, but this requirement will be initiated by the actions of others, not ours."

The jokers drove into the heart of their little town and parked in their colored assigned parking space. They slowly climbed out of their truck while moving as non-threateningly as they possibly could. They made sure that they recognized every person they got close enough to without having to talk much above a whispers.

Buck led the other two through the door of the burger joint and led them politely to a seat. Buck finally got up and went to order for all.

"Afternoon Miss. Wells. How are you this fine afternoon?"

"What do you boys want, Buck?"

"We would like three hamburgers with everything on them, that is if you have time to fix them."

"Go back and have a seat and I will call you when they are ready."

"We thank you with all our hearts, Miss Wells. We sho will be setting right over here waiting. Thanks Miss. Wells."

The deputy sheriff was sitting outside waiting for the craziness he thought was to begin. Instead it was one of the most peaceful days that anybody could remember. The word had been spread to the whole colored population to play dead and remain indoors until the hostilities slacken. The colored people were well aware that they would not stand a remote chance of winning a head-on encounter with an angry and insane pack of hillbillies.

"Okay Buck, Your burgers are ready. Come on up here now before one of my customers comes in. That will be forty six cents."

"Now you boys got what you came in here for so you may go."

"No mam, Miss Wells. It's windy outside so we thought it would be okay with you if we were allowed to eat our burgers inside. There is a lot of sand blowing around out yonder. We know a nice Miss. Lady like you wouldn't want us to get sick from eating sand."

"Listen you boys. When did a little sand make colored folks sick? Y'all don't want to cause me any trouble do y'all?"

"No ma'am, Miss. Well. We sho don't want to cause a nice lady like you not a flyspeck of trouble. No ma'am, we don't want to do that just for a little thing like eating our burgers inside out of the weather. 'Fore we go, can we have a cup of water?"

"Are these here ….uh uh boys trying to start trouble miss Wells?

"I don't know what to make of them. They aren't sassing or nothing, but."

"No suh Mr. Deputy Sheriff. We wouldn't think of trying to start trouble in this here nice cafe."

"I think you boys have played yo games long enough for one day. So, lets get your butts out of here before you really have a game to play. Let's git!"

"Let's go men. Mr. Deputy has spoken and we sho don't want no trouble with the Law. No suh, not in a million yeahs."

"We sho don't Mr. Buck! We is sorry that you thought we were trying ta make trouble, no ma'am, not us."

"The new kind of men had passed the introduction to what was to come. They felt that the beginning was more than a simple success but a big "hallelujah!" for the time being. Here were Blacks scattered all over the back alleys waiting to see some black heads getting cracked. There were disappointed people on both sides of the boarder.

"I don't want to have to lock you boys up today, So, why don't y'all git fur home and let this be a lesson for you.?"

"Mr. Deputy!"

"Yea boy, what's the question?"

"Could you do us a tiny favor befo we go?"

"Go on! What in hell do you want now. Haven't you misfits wasted enough of my time?'

"Could you see your way to walk into de bank wid us? You are the nicest deputy dat we eva had. We is a bit nervous with all dem folks a looking in our direction. We have a deposit to make."

"Darn if this don't beat all. Come on let's go before I change my mind."

"Thank ya suh, Mr. Deputy. We won't forgit how nice you waz today."

Buck figured this was the only way they would be safe from the mad mob of Whites while walking in the front door of the bank. Buck knew the deputy would not insist that they go to the back door and be with them while he herd them into the empty bank through the back.

"Thank ya Mr. Deputy. We sho appreciate yo company. You have yoself a nice day now, ya heah?"

The confused and angry deputy didn't bother with acknowledging what the uppity Blacks said. He was to busy observing the looks of pure pride on the faces of the Blacks and the pure confusion on the faces of the Whites. The poor deputy will have a hard time explaining this unusual event to himself, or anybody else, for the rest of his life.

"The crazy three black men could not hold their feeling much longer. They had to get to the colored quarters as quickly as possible so they could celebrate their victories in style. They felt like they imagined true heroes would feel. There was nothing like doing something about their being treated wrongly for no other reason than a birth mark.

The people in the quarters thought these three had gone completely out of the little minds they had. The men were seen doing all the new dances of the time. They were dancing in the streets, on the porch of the lounge and right through the door.

"Hey y'all up in here! Praise the Lord! Hallelujah! God is doing his thing! Hallelujah!"

"What in in the world ails you fools?"

"Where have you been, J.W.? You must have been over in Alabama buying your cheap rot gut when we were uptown becoming heroes."

"Yeah, I heard something like this was about to take place,

but I didn't think for a minute that you fools would carry it off. Here is a pint of my best stuff and it's on me."

"What do you men think of our way of getting the attentions of the whole town, except J.W.'s?"

"It takes some men with loose screws in their heads to pull this on our good sheriff and his deputy. Once they catch on you men won't be welcome nowhere.'

Nappy, how long have you been hanging around these kinds of places listening to our people grumble about not being able to speak their minds?"

"Every since I left home and learned that this would be about all I could hope to git to take care of me."

"You take care of these kinds of places where our men come to drown their miseries in. Places that sold J.W.'s kind of bad whiskey and green beer. You see it all the time. Now what do you really think that we did wrong, or foolish.?"

"I stopped trying to reason with most folks I know years ago. I accept everybody for what they is. You see I don't have a wife and children. I'm alright with what y'all is doing."

"Okay men, let's don't get too excited now because we have just got started. We have a lot of work to do yet before people like Nappy here can stand up straight and look folks in the eyes and tell them what's on his mind without being scared of getting his butt kicked."

"Buck! Getting Nappy to that mental state might take two or three lifetimes. Right Naps?"

"You boys go on and don't mind me. I'll be here long after most of you will be pushing up daisies."

"That is probably right Nappy. You have already buried a bunch. How many graves have you helped dig, Nappy?"

"I don't count them, Buck. I just help bury them. That's all."

"Okay boys, we have more work to do before sunsets. It will be less dangerous now that the people know we ain't gonna kill all their women and children and barbecue them."

"Fred, don't you feel like having J.W. and his helper here, who is Naps, throw us one of their leftover barbecue sandwiches our way?"

"Sounds good to me. Hand me that bottle over here. We might as well empty it so that J.W. can have his bottle back. After all he did give us the happy juice."

"You are right on the nose Bud. Come on you guys and let's get the boy his empty bottle back."

The popular men finished celebrating their success and came down out of the clouds and thought they would strut back up town while the crowd was still there. They knew that their safety was in the hands of the crowds.

The men didn't want to become known and accepted as just another few fools who could be ignored after being thrown into the social loony bin. The soldiers had to keep bringing on new approaches every day. They were about making lasting eye-openers to the people every day.

"Alright men, let's continue our crusade for what is rightfully ours. We can't let little small successes get in the way of us going for the complete package of goodies."

"You need some gas don't you Fred?"

"We can get five gallons while we are in town. I like to keep this thing with gas in it in case I have to get you law-breakers out of the country."

Mr. Jason didn't blink an eye when the men pulled up to the station. He stood behind the county while several loafing white men stood staring at Buck."

"I'm not gonna bite you Mr. Jason. We like for your man, Wilbert, to pump us five gallons of high test gas, if that's alright with you, Mr. Jason?"

"You heard what he said, Jason! Git out there and pump him five gallons of high test gas."

"I think we would like three coca colas too. Wait a minute.

Are those fresh moon pies? Give us three of those. That is if you don't mine."

Mr. Jason threw the pies on the counter and told Buck and Bud to get their own coca colas. The other men standing around chewing tobacco never saying a word. But, you could tell that they were keenly watching Buck's and Bud's every move.

"Buck are you gonna include this what we are doing now in your sermon that you will preach Sunday? What we did today will keep the members on the edge of them hard benches."

"How do you feel right now, Bud?"

"I'm riding high. I have never enjoyed seeing expressions more than I did today. These folks were looking at you and Fred like they had never seen y'all before."

"They hadn't seen the Fred and me that they were watching. Even we hadn't seen us behaving the way we were acting today. That is our mission. We have got to train ourselves and our people to see and treat us in a different way than what they normally do."

"Fred was walking on cloud nine once he knew we were not gonna be lynched."

"Fred might be ridding high on more than what we have gotten away with. He was taking some giant swallows of that corn liquor."

"I'll see y'all in the morning. We need some cash to be happy fools. See you at the church house tomorrow."

Buck and Bud have to get to work on a super good presentation at church. This changing minds about who and what is will be a major step on the journey to where these boys thought they wanted to be. They had something to go on with what they had learned in town. The job of changing the other people's minds was the easy part. Changing their own people's minds about who and what, might be the tough project. These men were beginning to believe that the other side was less responsible for the Blacks being short-changed than the Blacks themselves.

CHAPTER NINE
CAUSE AND EFFECTS

"We better git going men. We don't want to keep the law waiting. These super humans don't like having to wait for us to get to our appointments. They think that they have done enough when they agreed to meet with us."

"Y'all finish eating your food. The Sheriff will be sleeping in his office all day, unless he gets a call. What do you boys think he would think of your time if he do get a call?

"He will have second thoughts after we git through with him. Otherwise, why are we wasting our times fooling with these marble heads."

"Maybe it's to make you feel better."

"I'll tell you something that we thought you already knew. I want to jump the broom before its too late for me to raise a few rug rats. Ain't that right Bud?"

"We've gone over this a hundred times. That's about all me and my forever-one have to talk about here lately."

"We are trying to make changes in this community's ways of treating people of color. I can't see myself crawling on my belly in order to feed a family. I want my wife and children to have a man to lead them down this rocky road called life."

"I still want to hold a grand child or two before I cross the bridge of no return."

"I believe you would cross that bridge of no return in a higher spirit if you knew that your grands stood a chance of living a better life than you had to live. I don't think my daddy would even dare to cross over before he knew we were on a better path than he walked."

"Yeah, but he did crawl off that high wagon and screw his right mind back in his head. You see him in the mirror every day, don't ya?"

"Good night grand ma wanna be!"

Buck drifted off to a restless sleep after lying awake for half the night thinking about what to do with the rest of his life. His mama, his pastor and a few of the white people advised him to rethink what he was attempting to do.

The church was full due to what the three rock-heads had started. The young men and women were at church not to hear the sermon, but to hear what Buck and his sidekicks had to share. That was the main reason that Buck was thinking of becoming a social maverick through the gospel. The Church was his weekly contact point.

"Morning my fellow members. I know you are eager to hear my report from my side about what happened in town yesterday. I am of the mind that God expects his children to do some work for themselves. I don't believe for one minute that God is gonna come down here and do for us that which we can so easily do for ourselves. Therefore we, when I say we I'm talking about Bud, Fred and me, decided we aught to get the ball rolling. This ball of social justice has to be kicked in our direction if we are to reap equal social benefits. We did play around with the minds of some of our smartest citizens. I want to share this finding with you.

I'll let Fred share his take with you before I give you mine. Fred will you come up here?"

"Good morning fellow members. I kind of had a hunch Buck was going to put me on the spot today. SO! I wrote out a few notes here so I would be able to remember something. I'm getting more and more confused every day about the whole situation. I have never paid this much attention to how our people think about themselves and us. I see now that we have a bigger problem than we thought. I was under the impression that we were dealing with a people who knew what they were doing and why. Folks, they have proven otherwise. We are trying to get a bunch of fools to see where they are wrong at. These folks, both Coloreds and Whites, think this is the way God planned it. What I'm telling you is the people who you think you are dealing with ain't the ones you think they are. These folks are strangers. So, get ready to deal with folks who you don't really know what's on their minds, or how they see you. That's all I have to say for right now"

"Y'all heard Fred's thinking on this mess we have to deal with. I'm asking all of you to include this mission we are on in your prayers. I can't see us getting to where we want to be without God's help. I know this don't sound too promising, but this is what I see coming our way. I'm gonna share something with you that might be an eye-opener. Our people really don't have any ideas of what it is that you want from them. They are under the beliefs that you, and themselves, are where God intended us and them to be. The first hurdle we'll have to jump is the ignorance on both sides about what it is we are trying to do. We would think that our people would realize that what is good for the goose is also good for the gander. We have to get the point over that what we do that's good for one we believe it will benefit the other. We are trying to make the whole United States a better United States by giving all its people a chance to partake. Our people seem to really believe that God didn't put enough goodies here for all his critters. Yeah Sammy!"

"I wonder where all these crazy notions come from. Were we born with the crazy idea that one people was put on earth to be servants to another. How do they answer questions like that?"

"Sammy, we haven't got their attention to the point that we could ask such a deep question. I haven't seen any evidence of these folks ever entertaining such thinking. They are so set in their ways until questioning their ways don't ever cross their minds. They figure we are interfering with God's plans when we get too close to bringing up the issue. Most of the Whites and a big chunk of the Blacks thinks that us three men should be locked up somewhere. They have a point in a way. We will be causing trouble because we want to change our ways of living and that includes all of us. But, there is always a price to pay for change, for the better or for the worse."

The tree men took mental pictures of the faces of the men and women packing the church to its maximum capacity. There was more fear and doubt shown than eagerness to do whatever was needed to bring about relationships that the men thought would result in their country and its people becoming the world's role model for how God expect people to treat each other.

"Buck, old T.J. got himself thrown in the slammer again today. He was in town clowning at the time that y'all were trying to pull the people together.'

"What was the old nut doing this time? I don't believe that T.J. don't know these folks by now."

"The rumor is that he was staggering down the front street singing at the top of his voice. He was behaving as if he had lost his cotton-picking mind."

"Bud, let's you and me go down to the sheriff's office and see what this is all about."

"Let's roll cousin. I think Fred will want in on whatever is. Don't you think so?"

"We'll drop by and pick him up."

The three warriors tried to make petty conversations as they rode toward the powers that they were sure to have to deal with. Each of the nervous men was trying to get a handle on the whys of this thing that they were going to face before the Sun went down.

"Good afternoon Mr. Sheriff! How is yo Sunday?"

"What in the hell are you boys wanting of me now? Ain't y'all done done enough to wreck my day?"

"No suh, we wouldn't do anything that we thought for a minute would spoil your Sunday, Mr. Sheriff."

"If you are here about that nutty T.J then you are wasting your time. I could not talk sense to the old man at all. He just might have to be put away until he regain the little sense that he had."

"Mr. Sheriff, could you see your way to let us talk to the poor nut?"

"You can waste all the time you want to. But it won't do you much good. Follow me."

Once the sheriff went back to his chair under the porch flap, the fun started. T.J. told his story which made all the sense in the world.

"Look you screwball, I'm in here because of y'all. The sheriff was all set to make an example out of some of you when I got the message. I thought that this was a good time for me to show how crazy I was. I did too. This took the sheriff's attention off what you folks were doing and he could show his folks that he was on the job by what he did to me. Don't y'all get the picture?"

"We do now. That was a beauty you pulled. We wondered why the old boy didn't show at the church. Plus the deputy up and drove off. We were wondering where you were also."

"Now you know. Somebody has to watch you crazy Negroes' backs. You know I have very little to lose by spending a few days living at tax payers expenses."

"I don't think you have to worry much about us three appreciating what you do. You make us look like boys playing children's games of marbles. But not for long. We will give you time for them not to blame you for what we will be up to once you get out of the slammer.

The fired up men started plotting their next mission. They wanted this attack to be much easier to understand by the common men and women. They had been giving folks too much credit for having good sense.

"Y'all know what my little gal wanted to know today?"

"No, we don't know. Why don't you tell us Harvey."

"She wanted to know if either of you three will be married by the time you men are too old to cut the mustard. You see I knew what she was driving at. She has been watching me hang around you folks."

"What answer did you give her?"

"I told her the truth about my plans. I told her to start getting ready to become Mrs. Harvey Winston. That's what I told her. You see we are not quite as old as you three but she could see how much I liked what Y'all are doing,"

"Tell her that we don't need any more like us out here acting like we are crazy. Three of us are plenty. We do want as many as we can get to start to refuse to play the dumb colored role."

"You men have more of us than you might think who will be ready to do what we think must be done to become full citizens of these United States."

The move was pull to a stop until old T.J. hit the ground as a free man. The men had rehearsed their next move for days.

Possibilities to work on making the world a better place to live and die in were raining down everywhere. There was chances to make a contribution toward making a positive difference in how man treated his fellow man at every contact man made with his fellow man. Some meeting offered greater opportunities than others.

"Mr. Ross sent us word by Daddy that he had some hard work for us to do. Let's ride up there and check this out. He has some of the best timber land in the county. His daddy wouldn't let them log it while he was still alive. What do you think Fred?"

"Like you said, he has some of the best timber in the county. We aught to know as much hunting we do on his land."

"Afternoon Mr. Ross! I got word that you wanted to see us. Here we are."

"Yeah, I told Sam to tell you boys to come and see me. I may have a deal for y'all."

"Like I said, here we are at your command."

"Come on around behind the house. I stopped feeding the chicken when I heard y'all old truck pull to a stop."

"We are right behind you, Mr. Ross. By the way, where is that old mean bitch of a hound at?"

"Don't worry about her. She is in the hen house with her new litter of pups. Y'all can sit on the edge of the porch while you listen to my offer."

"We are all ears, Mr. Ross. We are cutting our last strip of pines this week."

"Let's talk about what you can do for me and I can do for you. I want to get some good honest and hard-working crews to work with me in stripping a track of my best wooded land. I believe you boys are more aware of how much timber I have over there than I am. You have trespassed in them woods enough to cut the trees blindfolded.'

"Aw shucks Mr. Ross. We was just trying to get prepared for what you are about to ask us to do for you. We were just making sure there was nobody else hunting on our land. You know how them boys from Alabama hunt. They will wipe out every living critter in them there woods in a few days."

"This is what I got. If you boys want to take this job on, you go back home and think this over, decide what and how you will do the logging and give me whatever y'all come up with."

"Thanks Mr. Ross. We be show to do that. You show have a

nice flock of chicken and ducks there. Let's get out of the man's way men and let him finish feeding his feathered friends."

The three soon-to-be rich men could hardly hold their excitement in until they were safely on the road home. They had to talk to somebody with more experience at these big jobs than the three of them had.

"What have you men come up with that will be fair to all involved? You know old man Ross tries to be fair enough so his conscious won't bother him. This is where you might be able to get a workable and fair-and-square deal."

"Daddy what do you think we should do to get at an impartial deal for all?"

"I suggest that you boy take a drive out to Big Rock tomorrow and talk this over with Roy Coleman. He has cut timber all over this state. He was and still is the money maker for the Harris over there. He'll know the upper and lower limits of what you can charge and not come out in the hole."

"That's our first move in the morning. We should be back before twelve and over at Mr. Ross's house. Let's git to bed Bud. We will be out of here before breakfast."

They got there lumber-jacking education from Roy Coleman. The senior lumber jack had been in the business since before people of color could have a say in how much or how little they got paid for their services.

The wheeler and dealers were at Mr. Ross's just at lunchtime. They had to wait until the landowner finished his spaghetti and meatballs.

"What did you boys figure out? Tell me what kind of deal you think you'll be able to live with and I'll see if I can live with it too. I want to be fair-and-square with all God's people. You are just as much God's creation as men like me. Don't you boys ever believe otherwise. You hear me?"

"Yes sir. We thought that around one third of the price the

wood is sold for will be fair to all. And that includes Bud and me using our own truck."

"What truck? I don't see y'all being able to do too much with that old trap you got."

"That is another issue we want to run by you. We have a solution for that. You see, if you could see your way to co-sign for a newer dependable truck we would all benefit. Bud and me will own the truck as long as we make the payments to the bank, or to you. How do that sound to you Mr. Ross?"

"Where in all God's creation did you boys get such an idea? Don't get me wrong now. It sounds like this nutty idea might work, but... I'll have to think about this for a few hours. Y'all come back in the morning."

The smart butt big-time black business men left their potential partner with full confidence that all would be just fine. They made sure that there was enough loose ends dangling to give the good white man the chance to make an offer that would appear to come from him. Any Black with common sense knew that a white man would rather lose his prized bull than accept a Black's idea of a good deal no matter how fair it was. Whites had no socially experienced concepts of what being fair to Blacks was from the Blacks' side.

"What do you think Fred? What will the big boy come up with?"

"What will he decide about the truck, or the share of the profits?"

"The total thing. He has a chance to change a lot. We gave him plenty room to wiggle around in. We would be fine with what we said which is a fourth of the money. We can get the truck without him if we have to, but this gives him a big say in what truck he will be signing for. He will also make the dealer believe that he is more in charge than he really is."

"What do you think he will come up with about the mules to drag and load the logs?"

"I'll bet he will offer his mules to us for that. This will give him some direct control over the operation. You see, the days work will have to began at his lot gate if he owned the muscles."

The next morning would be slow coming around so the boys decided to grab a gut settler from their favorite porch rooster; the moonshiner.

"Afternoon Mr. Ross!" Buck greeted Mr. Ross."

The two sidekicks never said a word.

"Come on around back here. I'll get us some good cold ice tea. Go right ahead and set yourselves down wherever you can find a seat,"

The hotshots didn't dare make themselves too comfortable before they knew what the old man was sugar-coating them for. Ice tea? The three men nerves started to tingle.

"Well now, I think I have worked out a good deal for all of us. I want you boys to listen with a business ear now. Business is done a bit different from working for a wage. We will have to figure out what the percentages are and to whom they go."

"Yes sir, we are all ears, Mr. Ross."

"This is the way my figuring came out. I will go with you boys to get the truck. I won't be responsible for it's maintenance or payments. Those will be your jobs unless you need to borrow a few dollars to buy tires or other high priced stuff Then I might see my way to loan you the cash at a fair interest charge. Do y'all follow me so far?"

"It' sounds better than what we could come up with, Mr. Ross."

"Now here comes the deal that all the others will depend on. I don't see your idea of getting a third of the profits. But, I do think a fourth is more than fair if I provide the team of mules. The mules will save you men a bundle with having to feed and make sure they are healthy. Well?"

"When can you be at the truck dealers? We have the truck already picked out and a deposit is on it to hold it until you get a peek at it."

"I'll go into town this afternoon. You boys won't have to

be there. My word will be just fine. You boys were pretty sure I would have a deal, huh?"

The men even got a bit more than they would have accepted. The cost to not feed the team would save them a bundle. Them big logging mules could eat the profits up. Plus, it cost to have a veterinarian to keep them in good physical shape. A veterinarians would cost a black man an arm and a leg. The same would be true for truck repair, tires and fuel. These expense were about half the usual cost if the dealers figured Mr. Ross was benefiting from the deals.

"What do we have here men? Can you see us making money?"

"The man has enough timber to keep us working for a long time. By the time we are finished with the first thinning out, it will be time to start over."

"What about the deal we got? What do you think Bud?"

"I don't believe we could have don any better going somewhere else. It is the best deal we ever had."

"Well, men, tell us what the deal was."

"Daddy, you and Mama were right. We threw out what we thought would give the old coon something to work on and he did. We got more than we bargained for."

"You followed my advice. I reminded you what would work on these people. If you know what makes a people tick, you will know what to do in order to get them to do what you want them to do. There is no secrets about what makes people do what they do."

"You are right about what is true today. But, I'm getting a bit fed up with playing these silly games. I am tired of having to act stupid for these nuts to do right by us. They don't have to do that with each other."

"I know what you are having to deal with, son. I just want you to know that whatever you decide to do with your life and how you live it, we are with you. We know you are not stupid at all. We trust that you will be fully aware of the cost of whatever dealing you do with our fellow citizens. They are only a part of the system. We are the rest."

"The way we have to get along with our fellow citizens makes me feel like the biggest fool that God created. I'm just sick of this craziness. I promised my self that this was the last time that I would play the part of an idiot in order to live in peace with these show enough idiots."

"Well you boys got a living made for a while to come. Thank God!"

CHAPTER TEN

CHAPTER TEN

BECOMING A STRANGER

Buck and the sidekicks were off on a different road to no-man's land. They had no clear picture of what it was that they lack to be complete, but they did know that their fool playing days were over.

"Men, what do y'all think about us taking a week off and do a little traveling, since we are members of the richest citizens in the area. We can afford to give our families a bit of the good things. Bud, I know you and your old lady need some fresh air. You have been married now over two years and haven't been further than Mobile with Daddy and me."

"Mae and I have been talking about you and what your plans were for your life,"

"We are in a position now where we are richer than the average member of the community which gives us opportunities that we didn't have in the past. I've got to decide what me and Rachel gonna do. I can't expect her to become an old spinster just because I don't have the guts to make a go out of what we have. If we don't go for ourselves now, when will we?"

"You have noticed Rachel hanging on to our little Buster every chance she gets. You know what that spells. I see you don't miss one chance to snatch him from us whenever we are within your arm's reach."

"I talked to the pastor just this morning about how much do he think God wanted us to sacrifice for family, etc. He was of the mind that God didn't want any of his children to deny themselves a normal life because of what somebody else do. He said that we all have to reap what we sow. This is what I've thought since I was in diapers."

"When are you gonna pop the question? If you wait any longer you'll be your children granddaddy instead of their daddy."

"Shut yo mouth talking that junk. I never had, and still don't have, any intentions of raising a family on my knees praying to a man who is shorter than I am in every way."

"I know this will take a load off Aunt's and Uncle's shoulders. They were beginning to think that you wanted to wait until you turned white before you two jumped the broom."

Buck had dreams of being the kind of black man that he had never seen before. All his kind of men who took the high roads to their being ending up paying a heavy price. They became unfit to be good for much of anything but trouble. Buck and his partners went by their favorite joint to get some nerve juice and plans their futures.

"I thought we would wake up some time in our lives and do what will have to be done. The handwriting is on the wall. This latest generation will never stand for doing their thing the old way. Even old T.J. can be a witness to that. But, we aught to go back to our old ways, men. Let;s get into some butts, because we are the leading Blacks in this area. We have it made and can't lose too much."

"Where and when do we get this show on the road. I have gotten a little bored with our easy ways of making ends meet. We haven't had much excitement since we confronted the deputy and darn near scared the poor green horn to death"

"Let's start with the ones we do business with every day. Let's have Mr. Ross explain why is it that we have to use the back porch when we socialize at his house, but he uses our front porch when he drops by our homes."

"Only you could have come up with such a good starting person. I want to see every frown on his face when you ask him the question."

"I thought it would be more sincere if we started this mess at home. You know what they say about cleaning up your house before going cleaning up somebody else house."

"We will have our chance to pop the questions to the god-fearing man this coming Saturday."

"I'll do the asking so he will be sure to understand what we are asking him to consider. He will be the man we can practice this new approach to equality on. You hear me don't you? I am going to start reading everything that I can get my hands on that relates to social equality."

Buck practiced his new approach to his head-on collision with the age-old accepted ways of doing business with the world he lived in. He ran the half-thought-out speeches by whoever he could get to lend him an ear.

"Daddy, how do you see Mr. Ross answering a question like this? Mr. Wilson what do you see wrong with all our children attending the same schools together?"

"Buck, let me ask you that question while you play the part that you are asking Mr. Wilson to play. Mr. Buck, what do you think about all children being educated in the same schools?"

"I see what you are getting at. We have to take under consideration Mr. Ross's community position. His answer will be based on what he sees that he is risking by how he answers the questions. His answer may not be exactly the same as he would say in front of blacks, whites, or mixed people."

Buck went to bed having second thought about what the problems might be with him and his boys 's plans. This social mix of people, who are free to have and be who and whatever, will hear questions differently than if everybody had the same things to gain or lose. He did not think about changing his mission, but changing how he will go about attacking the way it is.

"Okay men. This is the showdown. I'm gonna start by asking this old boy some easy questions. I'm gonna ask him to give us his opinions on a few changes that are less of a threat to him and his."

"Afternoon Mr. Ross! How are you on this beautiful afternoon?"

"It sure is a beauty. This weather reminds me of when I was a boy and Mother let us play outside with our wagons and tricycles."

Mr. Ross did not answer the question that was asked. He also did not ask any questions of Buck and crew. Buck asked him how was he doing.

"Mr. Ross! What would you think if our board of education combined our colored and white schools and all the children went to school together?"

"Would you repeat your question? I didn't understand the question. What is it that you are asking?"

"What do you think about us just having one school and let all the children attend together? Do you think the county and the state would save money?"

Buck thought he would put the question in a text with money as it's foundation and see if the man would hear better. Making money was a skill that the man had and could think about while overriding many other minor subjects.

"I have always thought that would save us a ton of money if only it would be good for the children. My main concerns would be for the little black children."

"What about the little black children that you are so concerned about?"

"Well, will these little wide-eyed tots have the ability to keep up with the Whites?"

"Why don't you think they won't be able to hold their own, that is if given a chance?"

"I don't claim to know all the answers, but, I am concerned about the realities of such a change."

Buck and his crew were getting the deep subconscious thinking of what their mission was facing. The more crazy irrational answers he received from his folks the more he became determined to put them on the spot. The men started to think about all the possible answers that was in the book. A few objections even made sense.

One question was on Buck's mind a lot and that was, do the Blacks really need to be taught by Whites? Another question was, were the two educations the same? These were serious questions.

"Men, let's sat down and see what this one school system would do for the Blacks. Would any one of you want to be in a room full of Whites and being taught by Whites? You know how much they outnumber us. What kind of day would we have sitting among a bunch of these white children?"

"You have a good point, Buck. Suppose two boys got in a scrap and went before the counselor who is most likely to be a White."

"This is what bothers me. The colored children would be made to feel even more like step- children than they do out here in the real world. There are two places that we can think of ourselves as blessed and are part of a good god's creation and those places are the black churches and the black schools. We might have to switch our questions to how we old folks are treated."

Buck and the men parked near a colored school to watch the children walk and play on their way home. They seemed to be so equal and detached from the ugly part of an unequally divided community services. They appeared to have no racial issues.

"Fred, what do you think about us involving our children in this fight that we will surely have on our hands.?"

"The children will be hurt if we put them on the front line. I have no idea which way would be the best for us all either."

"Let's think about ways that will not involve the innocent

any more than necessary. We will have to think of some ways to crack the heads of the guilty and these guilty may include as many of us as it do them."

"We were on the right track all the time. We were having fun doing this thing too."

"We know you were having the time of your life T.J."

"I have always operated above and beyond the children. When I challenged a belief or action, it was where the innocent would be less likely to be hurt. You men know that. This is why we have to go after the old white and black community leaders. There are culprits in both camps."

"That you have. We can give you that much credit. You were way ahead of the crowd of your day and maybe ours too. Tell us T.J. where would you go from here.?"

"I would continue what you men started out doing. You should do it in a more businesslike way instead of for fun. I know how much fun it is to play fools for what they are, but we want to accomplish more than fun. Your position is needed now and has been for as long as I can remember. You said that you would get on your knees for God only. You would never again play the fool game to please a man, never again."

"I don't see us playing a game doing nothing but making all parties to it guilty of a serious crime. That crime is committing acts that make all of us mentally crippled."

"Buck nearly runs the church and he does a fine job too. Our pastor would not be as powerful as he is without Buck being on the deacon board."

"Thanks Bert. You have seen a lot more than we have and based on what you know, where is the weakest side of this mess? Where should we start.?"

"It has already been said, start at home. You see I came back home."

"You mean for us to forget the other side of this problem and consecrate on our own people who will need plenty eye-openers."

"You got it Mr. Smith."

"Mr. Bert, how would you like to join our little movement?"

"I would like that. Thanks for asking me. Maybe this will give me something to make me feel like a man. There are times when I curse God for bringing me into this world as a black man."

"Did you hear Mr. Bert, men? You see we have people waiting in line to join us. We must have a mission worth working toward and will benefit most of the community. Let;s each ask at least two men or women to join us."

The movers and shakers had a crew of fifteen or more recruits before the Sunday's service came to an end. They were proud of themselves for the small step in the right direction they were making. This direction was clear in their minds anyway. They would soon learn even more than they already had learned that their right might be wrong from the point-of-view of others.

Buck and Bud called a mid-week meeting of all the newbies to get them in tune for the coming Sunday after service get-together. They wanted to give these new men some printed materials to read so they would be ready to answer questions relative to what their goals were. They would be able to answer questions that their families might lack good informed answers to.

"Men it appears that we will have to train ourselves before we can expect to influence changes in others to get their help in accomplishing our mission. Let's start with you J.B. How would you answer this question. What is it you men are wanting from us? Let's say this came from a white man. What would be your answer, Mr. J. B.?"

"I would say that we want to have the rights to vote."

"That's one answer. Bert, how would you answer that same question?"

"I would tell him that I wanted the same rights and privileges as he had. I would be looking the dummy square in the eyes while I inform him that I will settle for nothing less than the social goodies that he and his family have."

"Bingo!! Did everybody get what Mr. Bert said? Do we know what it really meant? I'll tell you what I take it to mean. He is saying that he didn't want more than was fair, but would settle for nothing less than what was there for all. He is saying that second class citizenship just will not cut it."

"Mr. Smith! Some of these people who are so used to getting their way will put up a fight. I can see my boss now "Don't you boys have it better than people in Africa?"

"My answer to that dumb response would be simple. I would turn and ask him the same question. Don't you have it better than people in Africa, Mr, Boss!"

"Great comeback. Are we together? Our jobs will be to take nothing less than what is available to all the people. If we are refused the best that this country has to offer when we have done nothing to be denied the best for, we will make a stink that can be smelled up to high heaven."

"Yes sir, you in the corner, uh. James I believe."

"You got it. I'm Mae Allice's son. What will we do when we are cussed out for wanting the same thing as everybody else?"

"James, you are a little young to get the total of what the problems are but, welcome aboard, son. When we are refused for no reasons other than our race, then we have a duty to do whatever is necessary to make the changes. Keep in mind son this one important thought, this is being done for you and the young more than it is for us who have already missed a lot by how we are treated."

"I understand. I have been talking to my cousins and friends and they too want to join y'all."

"That is music to our ears. You see y'all will have to continue where we leave off at. You tell them young whippersnappers to hold their positions because we will need them later."

Buck, and his army, geared up for the spring season when everybody and his brother would be out and about. This was a good time to get the ball rolling at full speed. The farmers, loggers and ranchers would be tooling up for what was prayed for and that was a beautiful and growing summer. Each member was sworn to uphold and promote the by-laws of the army of justice seekers. They were to take nothing less than what was offered to the majority of the population's members.

"Listen for a minute men. We will have to keep a sharp eye on what prices are paid by the Whites and compare them to what we are charged for the same services. This will be our starting point. We all know how to do that little demand. Are we ready?"

The social slaves made themselves ready for the slaps and kicks that they were sure would be coming their way. Business of this kind required unlimited practice and patience. Every encounter with the resisting brothers and sisters would need to be handled a wee bit differently than the last one. The men decided to start the initial new attacks at the local business levels.

"Alright you two heroes, let's get in here and get things churned up. We should be good from the results of the long hours we've been beating this over the head."

"All you have to do is lead the way."

"Thanks Mr. Marshall. You didn't have a second thought about sticking me out front."

"I had no thoughts of pointing at somebody else. You are the only one of us with the gift to speak the two languages plain enough to be understood by all."

"Let's get the ball rolling. Come on let's go spend some money. Mr. Evans is waiting for us to come in so he can make a profit. He has a family to feed."

"We are right behind ya. Get on through the door, captain!"

"All right, just don't push me. We have to be cool as a cucumber, Mr. Marshall."

"What can I do for you boys?"

"Neither of the near middle-aged men responded."

"What's the matter with you boys? Did the cat get y'alls tongues?"

"Did y'all hear something, Bud? Marshall?"

"Nothing that was said to us. There must be some invisible little people in here somewhere."

"Well! If this don't beat all hell. Have you boys gone and loss y'alls cotton picking minds?"

"I still hear that funny noise ringing in my ears. Let's ask Mr. Evans do he hear that racket."

"Mr. Evans, can we get some help down here?"

"Well if this don't beat all. What do you boys want?"

"There is that noise again about boys. I don't see any boys in here. Mr. Evans are you talking to us. I don't see no boys in here.?"

"Who else is in my store? Do you see anybody else in here?"

"No, but I heard you say how could you help some boys. Do we look like boys to you, Mr Evans?"

"What is y'all's point? Are you b,,, folks trying to start trouble?"

"Not on your life. We thought you was trying to git a rise out of us. I'm sure if one of us referred to you as a boy there would be feathers flying ever which way."

"I think you b— folks have been drinking something strong. I suggest you all go somewhere and sober up and then come back after you have regained your right senses."

"No sir, Mr. Evans, that won't happen. This is the new times and you might as well get used to doing business with the new us. Do you get the picture, Mr. Evans? You will have to get it if you want to continue doing business in this part of the county."

The men thought it had come time to vacate Mr. Evans property. They felt satisfied with what they had done thus far. The store owner looked as if he would have a heart attack at any time.

"These white folks are pitiful. I believe that some of them would rather be dead and buried in their graves than to treat us as equals. What do you think Fred?"

"It won't be easy for them to change how they see us. We

think we have a problem adjusting to the new us, you see what these old boys gonna have ta deal with."

"Let's git down to the church, men. Let's see what some of the others have to share with us."

Buck and crew knew something had gone terribly wrong when they saw the lights flashing on top of the sheriff's prowl car.

"I was getting tired of waiting for you, Buck and your trouble makers, I want you to tell me what do you men think you are doing? I hope you noticed that I addressed you all as men. What is it that you want from a bunch of innocent people who have done nothing wrong to you folks."

"Sheriff, would you allow me to play a little game with you? Then maybe you will get the idea of what this is all about. Would you let me play a game with you?"

"I don't have any idea what it is you are after, but go on."

"Tell your deputy to be calm and don't get jacked out of shape. Now let's get started. I'm gonna ask you a simple question Sheriff. What in hell are you two boys doing out here this time of the day? Huh? Don't you boys have other important jobs that you could be doing? Do you hear me talking to you boy?"

"Sheriff! I can cuff em for you."

"Hold up deputy. Buck do you know you just gave me reasons to place you under arrest?"

"For what Sheriff?"

"For getting out of your place and disrespecting me and my deputy. Did you hear how you were talking to me, your sheriff?"

'I sure did. The same as you and the deputy were addressing us. Did you folks hear yourselves?"

"How was that Mr. Buck?":

"Now you are getting the picture. You just addressed me like you will have to from here on or I won't pay you any attention. Do you hear me, Mr Sheriff?"

"All I can tell you and your trouble making crew is don't let me catch you folks in town carrying on with your silliness. Do you folks hear me?"

"Sheriff! Sheriff! Do you know who you are talking to? We are your new people who you are gonna have to protect from your own kind. You see your duty is to see that men like us will be free to participate equally in the dances of freedoms."

"Buck, I don't believe that our boy have any ideas of what it is that you are telling him. Do you Mr. Sheriff?"

"My daddy would have a fit if he was here to hear this kind of disrespect coming from folks like these. I don't know what in hell this world is coming to."

The sheriff was talking more to himself and his dead white folks than he was talking to Buck and three or four nobodies.

"Men I do believe that the poor sheriff has had enough for now. But don't give up on this fine fellow. He just might go and spread the word about you crazy black folks."

"I hope you are right Fred. But, that is asking much from a man who has been trained all his life to see thing only one way and expect this same man to suddenly change the way he sees the things that control his everyday being. But, that's his problem."

"Hey men, we have time for another head-cracking. Where from here, Buck?"

"Slow down Mr. Marshall. Rome was not built in a day, so that's the saying. Let's take this apart and see it from all sides. That dance you saw the sheriff do is nothing compared to what we will be seeing from here on. That is, if we don't get our brains beat out."

Buck and crew became strangers in their own community and among people whom they had known all their lives. The mix of people started to avoid them whenever they were in the public's eyes. This avoiding behavior was for good reasons too. It seemed to be trouble where ever members of this crowd happened to be.

CHAPTER ELEVEN

FULL SPEED AHEAD

The civil rights of all Americans were beginning to enter the minds of the average people and they began asking serious questions. People were learning to read, watch the news and put two and two together and come up with some ugly pictures of our cockeyed social system. At least that's what they were being fed by the news media and gossiping grapevine.

"Mr. MacDonald call me and wanted to do some very serious business. He is finally ready to cut the strip of timber up there in the horn swamps."

"Buck! Do you know where his land is?"

"I sure do. It'll take a lot of good dry weather and months of road-building to even get to the beginning of his woods. This is what I wanted to tell you kinky heads. He wants us to use the crew that we have, use the tools we have and buy our own mules and do the work for less than we get from these white folks. Do you hear what I'm saying, men?"

"Ain't no way! Who do he think he is, or better yet, who do he think we are?"

"I'm coming to that. Just bare with me for a minute before y'all go over there and hang the rascal. Now listen to this. He said that the average one of our men could live on a lot less than they do. He looked me directly in the eyes when he accused me of being too concerned about the poor Negroes who ain't got sense enough to use money wisely anyway."

"I hope you got that skunk told off. Who in the dickens do he think we are?"

"I couldn't knock him too bad because he put me in the same category as he put himself. He was not talking about me. He was talking about you ignorant and empty-headed Negroes. He told me that the reasons why I didn't have even more than I have is because I'm too soft on you colored trash."

"I know you got the horned lizard told. I would have loved to hear what you had to say to that uncle tom."

"Like I said earlier, I kind of liked his way of educating me. I didn't realize that you men have been my worst enemies. You men have robbed me of millions. You folks should be ashamed of y'all selves. He told me that he and I were not to be tied to people like y'all and to work with people more on our levels."

"You know why he might have been testing you out don't ya?"

"I show do. His crew of misfits could never be able to operate in them kinds of woods and live to tell about it. He wants a crew who is capable of getting the job done, but he wants this new crew to do the work for the same cost to him as the others did. He is right too, We can do the work at a reasonable cost to him and his and use his chosen folks he wants me to give the best jobs to. The pay we pay his snails will come out of you men's cuts,"

"You don't have to use the dirty words that we know you included in the speech you unloaded on the man. No sire, we won't ask you to repeat the language again for our nice Christian ears. But, tell us in a nice way the guts of how you told that old uncle tom off!"

"All I told him was that I would gladly pass this offer on to you men and go by what you men wanted to do. I told him that

I could never in one lifetime tell him what you men would say. No sir, I'm too nice of a man to think I can speak for you men."

The crew had themselves a big laugh over the offer from the Mr. MacDonald. The Mr. MacDonald was an example of the other people that the average people of color had to fight in order to get out of the gutters. It was a common held belief that these kind of Negroes were the biggest problems the Blacks had to solve. As long as the Negroes had these kind of folks in their families it let the Whites off the hook of having to feel like the worst of the worst people to the colored folks. They could always point fingers at how bad the colored people treated each other.

"You know what that told me, men! I have to change who I'm pointing my fingers at a bit. The other side is still guilty of not treating their fellow men as they would want to be treated, but that don't give us the freedom to copy-cat their practices. What I'm suggesting men is let's don't let up on our original mission, but add more pressure to what we will be putting on our own kind, or suppose to be our own kind. Let's think about how we might shame these folks into rethinking their thoughts about who is who. We can have a little fun once in a while, can't we?"

"These kinds of Negroes need to be lynched on a public scaffold. These snot-nosed bastards give us more trouble than the others side."

"Marshall, Marshall! We owe these folks something. They are parts of us. Why don't we try and show them how they are seem from our points of view. Let's give them an image of themselves as shown through the eyeballs of their own kind. We will make a joke out of them. We will show them how they became the jokers that they are today. We want them to realize how foolish they are by trying to copy the habits of people who are their children and women worst social enemies."

"Old Marshall is ready to string the McDonalds up and all who he sees as being like them. Marshall, wouldn't that make us lower human beings than the Whites are? We will be lynching our own kind. At least the Whites try their best to stretch our necks most of the time rather than wiping out their own cousins."

"I know there is nothing more disgusting than one of your own thinking that another people is better deserving than his own with the same input. That is why we have to be careful that we don't become just another race of human's monsters. But! We will still have to keep a foot in their behinds. I realize that we are part of the problem."

"Men! Our partner here who we call Mr. Marshall is a natural born killer of white folks. We do need his kind but we will have to keep him on a leash until the time is right to do a bit of pecker-wood hunting."

"Buck thinks that how the Whites treat each other is their problem and the way we treat each other is our problem and the two should be kept apart."

"Fred is right about that one. If we mix these two human problems together we won't get to first base. We have a big enough job with what we are taking on right now. Now, let's get back to introducing ourselves to our partners in crime. Gentlemen! We are gonna have to hit these folks where it hurts and that is in their pockets. We are not going to continue to do their work and come out holding the short end of the stick. How do that sound to you?"

"I'm about desperate enough to try anything as long as it will get us to where we can be men, and respectable men at that."

"Marshall, you are one of us who comes close to having some kind of respect from all. We don't want to have too much of that kind of respect. They give you the kind of respect they give to what they believe are crazy n,,,,s. Uh, colored people."

"I learned by accident that being a crazy Negro is better than being a dumb one. There is nothing that makes me sicker than standing watching one of our great men be treated as if he was a dunce,"

"Believe me gentlemen, we will get more respect by doing

our thing in a respectable way. We will take every opportunity we run into and give whoever we are doing business with the upmost respect. This practice can start right here among us. Don't that grab you in your Christian hearts?"

"You sound like you have a plan all worked out, Buck. Let's hear what you have dreamed up in that reasonable and just mind of yours."

"I've been thinking about how we go about our mission. We usually have to wait until the other side do something that gives us reasons to lash out. Why don't we plan actions that are based on what we want, think and do? Let's put the other side on the spot and make them react to what we do, how do that sound to y'all acorn-headed men?"

These trail blazers were finally getting their actions more within their own control. This made it much easier to plan and carry them out.

"I'm writing out my Sunday speech to address just this approach. We will teach our people to behave like men and women at all times. We are to stay as far away from appearing to be hypocrites as we possibly can. There is nothing more phony than a person's actions that are not based on his/her true selves, It's hard to believe what you hear and see that we do every day. Even a stone fool can see through the crap that we feed ourselves."

"Maybe we do the silly bull to fool people into seeing us as something that we ain't because we are not proud of who we really are. I try to be something even if it do not fit what folk like to see."

"Yeah, we know you do, Marshall. You have proven beyond a shadow of a doubt that one can build his/her own public image."

"He sure has, but I don't believe that I want his kind of public image. I want to raise a few children who will have good sense and stand a good chance of becoming good citizens."

"Look Fred, I can see what the old man is talking about. Do we stand a chance of raising a mentally healthy family and be the kind of men who our young men and women can use as role models."

"The time will come when we will be able to be like everybody else, but that time is not here yet."

"That is exactly what we are beating our brains out trying to make happen. But, in the meantime, these men have to continue doing God's will."

These were the kind of discussions that these trailblazers had to have among themselves. They had made some progress but not nearly enough to make the treatment of people of color equal to that of the other ethnic groups in the south. There were times when these men thought about saying to hell with the whole idea of social equality. But, those notions were short lived and soon frittered away.

"What did you folks get out of the long sermon today?"

"I'll say one thing, he covered us all. I'm glad you asked the question, Bert. The pastor was generating more questions than he was giving answers to. What do you think Bud?"

"None of his congregation could come close to answering the kinds of questions he was asking. I really don't believe he had the fixes for the problems that he was making us aware of."

"Bert! All of the citizens may be aware of the absence of solutions to what ails our society. We don't have any history of our kind of problems being solved, or even existing in other parts of this big old world of ours. Like we have talked about before, we are gonna have to start from naught. This is our biggest problem. We have to figure out a way to address what we see as preventing us from getting out of this county what we think that we deserve."

"Well, you and bud go home, talked this over with your daddy and mama and bring whatever y'all figure out back to us. I'm kind of fed up with trying to get through to these brothers and sisters of ours."

"I get what you are feeling, Bert. I'm for treating them

buggers the same way they treat us. Let's give them some of their own medicine."

"Marshall, Marshall! We know how you would handle this thing. You just might have the only, or the best way of getting the point over. You know what they say, give them some of their own bull."

"Marshall, What we are trying to do is get something going where we all will be winners, not losers. Which side wins when warfare is going on in their own house?"

"You are coming close to what this country would be after the battles were over and it was time to rebuild. Would we have anything left better than what we had? What lesions would we be teaching our children? There has to be another way to wake up a sleeping population and get the members to do what is best for all."

"Deacon Smith, you have been reading the man's Bible too much. You folks gonna have to wake up and realize that most of our people don't a bit more believe in the holy words than a mule do. We will have to hit these folks where they live. In there homes and pockets is where these people live."

"That's exactly right, Marshall. But, and this is a big but, we can win this war if we use our heads first long before we crack heads. When it comes to head-cracking time the whole world will have to know whose faults the end results was. The fools who are fighting for inequality and denied justice to their brothers and sisters will be the culprits."

"Well, let's don't just sat around talking about it. Let's do something. I'm getting to the point where I'm hating myself for putting up with this crap."

"Bud and I will see you men tomorrow night right here at the hall. Put your thinking caps on and come loaded with ideas of the actions we will be deciding on."

The time was nearly right for big social changes that might

put the United States in a position where other countries could see it as something other than a hypocrite.

"Buck, you and Bud have been pretty quiet these past few days. What's in them there nappy heads of y'all's?"

"Mama! I don't really know. I'm beginning to see man as the biggest mistake that mother nature made when she created all the critters on earth. I'm beginning to think that we are the devil. I was talking to old man Willie yesterday about what all men should be given by their fellow men and he looked like I was speaking a foreign language or something. You know what he asked me?"

"We can guess what he was thinking. He was wondering if you had lost your cotton picking mind. He and I have had words before when your mama and me tried to do business with the old bigot."

"You know what he said? He said that God's plans were being carried out. He thinks that this is the way the good Lord intended for it to be. He said that the boys who were lynched over in Alabama was a sign from God for us to accept the way God had created this country of ours. He said there was nothing wrong as far as God was concerned. He said if what we thought and is trying to change was God's way it would have changed a long time ago, or would never have been in the first place." Can you believe him?"

"Yes we can believe he would have that kind of mind. How could he believe anything else and be a church-going Christian?"

"That's is what I'm beginning to question. How can man blame God for what man do to man. If God was responsible for the ills of mankind then we are all innocent of wronging our fellow men. There has to be more to it than using God as an excuse for man's sins."

"It is believed by most of the religious folks that God will bring justice and righteousness in his own time. He will forgive those who have not obeyed his commands"

"This coming Sunday's talk will be about righteousness in the eyes of God. There are others who have these same unasked and unanswerable questions in their minds. I wonder why we don't insist that our religious institutions address this problem.'

"It may be because others don't see what you see as questions to be asked. Our religious leaders might have all the justifications they want, or need, to be comfortable with what they think they know."

"I see we have more work and more work the further we get into this equality thing. Have we got to rebuild the mental world of all mankind before we cam expect him to do the right things?"

"As you, and others know I was once filled with them same kinds of ideas. But, I saw that if I wanted a fulfilled life here on earth I had better get rid of them lofty minded notions. I'm not saying that you have to give up on people doing what's right, but you have to forgive them for doing wrong."

"I guess you and all the rest of mankind are right. I don't see too many others who are worried about God participating in this war-dance between his critters over what he put here for man to share. I'll have to get busy helping my people make do with what is, instead of putting notions in their heads that make their lives worst than they are."

"Get yourself a good night's sleep and then think about what your Sunday's talk to the young men will cover. Talk what these smart country boys and girls can understand. Are you hearing me son?"

"Yes Daddy. I already know what your answers is. You give the same answers as the rest of our churches' seniors, even though you know better. You might not know what to do about this professed beliefs of ours, but you don't buy into the traditional bull either."

"Good night son. May your head clear by morning."

Buck had a mighty dream after the talk with his dad. He had to figure out whether the dream was from the good angels or the bad angels. Buck would have a heart to heart talk with his brain pool. He didn't share his dream with his mama and daddy. He told Bud about it on the conditions that he kept it to himself.

"Listen up you men! I have some serious questions for you all to consider and think about within the next few weeks. The first question is, do you believe that God was and is fair to all his created critters? These critters include all of his creations. Where do you get your food from? Do you believe that the condition of man has anything to do with the justice of God? Do you think that we are our own worst enemies? You guys don't try to answer them questions right away. Let them simmer in them dumb heads of y.all's for a few nights while you are snoring loud enough to keep the angels awake long enough to give you some hints."

"But, what have you gone and dreamed up now?"

"Well Fred, I'll keep my dreams to myself for right now because I have a lot of questions to ask myself. Whatever we come up with we will have to put into practice. We will have to assume a lot more responsibility for the human condition than we have thus far. Don't you think fellows?"

They all went their separate ways with a promise to the gang and themselves to ponder the questions and come up with something. What they thought they would come to terms with would not be the final trip into no-man's land, but a start.

CHAPTER TWELVE
Transformation

The South was waking up to some trues that had been keeping it in a backward state for hundreds of years. It was being depicted across the airwaves as being the butt of the America that was known throughout the known world. It's citizens had begun to travel and educate themselves. They were no longer ignorant of how people lived in other parts of their world. The people whose eyes were coming open were the men and women of color.

"Mr. Smith! What can I expect from you and your men within the next two weeks?"

"Now Mr. Ross, you know as well as I do that it will depend on the weather and my men being able to stand up to the task. You can get ready for all that the good Lord will bless us with."

"I show hope you finish up before the fall weather get here. That part of the county is muddy and slippery as lime rock is during the rainy seasons. The almanac is predicting bad weather starting in October."

"Mr. you might be able to control many things but the weather ain't one of them. As long as my people do their best, or close to it, we, and you, will be all that God expects us to be.

That's enough for me and my men. What else in the world do you want? Some of you folks makes me sick with yourselves."

"I didn't mean to get you started preaching. I just wanted to know how many railroad cars to order,"

"You'll have to get your answers from God."

Buck and the men were tooling up to give it all they had but not for the satisfaction of the old cripple land owner. There were times when Buck remembered his dying daddy's last words. "Son don't expect too much from your fellow men. They are just men." Buck would smile when he could feel the presents of his daddy and mama still guiding him through the storms of life.

"Bud! Would you and Fred go over and walk through Mr. Ross's woods and make sure that you come up with accurate figures. Check out them old logging roads while you are at it. We might have to clear new roads or to extend the old roads further into them swamps."

"We'll be on the job early in the morning, even in this here rain. It's suppose to clear up by the weekend, so the weather man said."

The old logging crew was aging faster than bananas get rip in the sun. It didn't seem like they had been doing business for over twenty-five years. They had to be careful when they gave out estimates relating to how much time was required to get jobs done. Their younger help could not be depended on to the same degree that the old members could be, back when.

"Mr. Ross gets more impatient the older he gets. It's about time for him to forget about what lay in the future. He is his future."

"I think he is trying to look out for that grandson of his. We all know that boy isn't worth two dead flies. The boy even flunked out of every school they put him in. He is one dumb white boy, if you ask me."

"Buck, you know who he blames that on? He told me that the schools lowered their demands for high quality education after the schools were desegregated."

"If that was the case his grandson should have been at the top of the class. When the truth is the boy could not keep up with the slowest students. But, this is the same old story of blaming all social wrongs on the people at the bottom of the social ladder."

"What is you and Rachel's plans for this coming weekend?"

"I don't think we have any set plans outside the usual. Why do you ask, Fred?"

"I don't expect you to remember our wedding anniversary when Rachel has a hard time making you remember yours."

"OPPS! I guess we will have to be there to help you celebrate your time in prison. That is if I want to live under the same roof with Rachel. You don't have to say more."

"Mae Wants everybody to dress up in their Sunday best because our son-in-law will be taking lots of pictures."

"That reminds me, is he still working for the same magazine that he was?"

"Yep, there is no other city like Chicago for publishing Negro papers. He says that if he could write for a paper here in the great state of Mississippi he would move back home."

"Has he ever thought about publishing his own paper? Somebody will do just that sooner or later and it might as well be one of ours."

"We have talked about this and he don't thinks there is a big enough reading population here to support a paper."

"We don't have to limit our paper to just our county. Ask him is there a way to sell the paper throughout the South and further if necessary. What make him think that his paper would be sold here only?"

"He is talking about when it starts up. The money to get started will be the problem. That's what he thinks anyway."

"Men, I have just got an idea about this paper thing. What would you men think of our giving our own a hand in getting something like this going?"

"It's something to think about. Then we could read our own news instead of reading about people a thousand miles away."

"It boils down to more than that, Ike. We would be able to tell our own story in our own way. The voice of the south's colored folks would be heard all over the country. Men, I think we have some work to do. Let's put our heads together bag up some help to offer the young man when he comes home this weekend. What do y'all say?"

The men who had run out of missions to help their people be recognized for what they were had stumbled upon another mission which would be just right for old minds. They would have a way to tell their stories through their own eyes and from their own black experiences.

Washington was at his in-law's party with his camera and photographing skills. He was planning to make a book thick enough to provide something to talk about with any company the old folks had. Washington had been a camera nut since the first Kodak Cameras came on the block.

"Mr. Washington, how have you been since the last time we talked?"

"Oh, about the same. I keep hoping it will get better but it stays about the same. I have been promoted since we talked but you know how that is. Getting a promotion in a company like the one that I work for wouldn't be much if you were promoted to the president's chair."

"We have an idea that you might like to think about. What do you think about owning your own magazine company?"

"What was that you said?"

"You heard me right. Think for a minute."

Washington had to take a few moments to get a handle on what he had heard. This was exactly what he had thought about all the way down the highways from Chicago to home.

"Did yo mention something about us starting our own Mississippi paper right here in our own little corner of the world?"

."I know it sounds like a crazy idea but it might be worth us giving it some thoughts. I know you have thought about this before now. How did the magazine company you now work for get its start?"

"Oh, I've heard the story a thousand times. The magazine was started by two dreamers who borrowed the down payment to buy a few desks and a printer. They were our present president and his deceased school chum."

"Then you already know that the idea is not so crazy."

"I drove all day yesterday thinking about the same idea that you got. What do you think would work here in your back door."

"Over where I went to college at they have their own paper and it keeps the locals informed. There is no reason why we can't do the same as they did. Let's give this some thought and see what we can come up with."

"When can we talk about this and with who?"

"You leave that to me. You go on back to your paper and let us old geezers look into what we need to get this thing on the road. This research will give us something to work on these white folks with. I will keep in touch with you. I will need your phone numbers, both home and work numbers, and some information about what is required and how much will it cost. Gather all the information for us and we will go from there."

"I'll get to work on that the first thing in the morning right after breakfast. I'll have to pick a few brains without them knowing why. It's hard to find people of color who can write a friendly letter, much less a newspaper article. Boy! This is the answer!"

"Have a good trip back home now. Drive carefully because you don't own yourself any more. You belong to your hometown."

Buck saw the height of the hill that was before them and it was steep. There would be obstacles by the dozens. He and his ancient boys would have a chance to get involved with the teaching of their fellow citizens a lesson. Buck had a brand new project to work on.

"Men, we have a brand new project to get going and this one is a beauty. Lend me your ears men!"

"I think I know what you are about ready to start. I saw you and Mr. Washington with y'alls heads together at the church yesterday. He looked offer pleased as he walked back to his fancy car. I figured you had told him something that he wanted to hear. We can guess what that something might be related to,"

"What about you Ike? What is your thinking on this big secret?"

"It wouldn't take a brain to figure out what you and Washington would have to talk about. Now go on and stop shucking and jiving and tell us what's on those educated minds of yours and Washington's."

"What do you men think about us having our very own news paper?"

"Wouldn't that be something. We would have a voice in this here community and this here state. Can you see these white folks faces if we had our own means of telling our stories our own way?"

"You are getting the point, Fred. We can make our own news which will be news that concerns us and those who might want to know what we are up to. I don't believe a true civilized community of people can be without some means of communicating on their own level and about the things that tells the stories of their own fussing people."

"How do you plan to get this sky-high notions of yours' in the air?"

"Mr. Washington promised to gather information relating to what is required and the cost that goes along with it. As he gathers this information, we will search the three counties in this area. We will need skilled personnel to get the job done in a big-time way. We won't settle for a mickey-mouse set-up. This will have to be first class."

"Where do we start at?"

"Hold your horses Marshall. We've got to take our time and make no mistakes. The powers will have to be left out of this completely. We want every move of ours to catch them boys off guard. You see they don't really think that we are capable of doing what we are planning. We can get the cash together on our own. We all know that we are the richest of all here in our necks of these here woods."

"It will be worth it to get a chance to show our people that we ain't the fools that we pretend to be and they think we are. I want to look in one of these big men face when I offer him a copy of the paper and tell him it's on me. Boy, we'll have what we need to put them monkeys in their places."

"Calm down Mr. Marshall. We won't only be putting the other guy in his place, but we will be teaching our own people where their places are. I think it might be more a tool to teach our own who we are than it will be to show the other guy who we are."

"It's the other guy that I will be eager to slap in the face. He has been brainwashing his people, and us, with the printed pages for years. Now it's our term."

"Don't worry about This madman here you guys. Me and Bud will get him on a short lease. There will come times when we will benefit by letting him run free, but we will pick them times. You hear that Marshall?"

"Maybe we would be further ahead than we are if men like me were given the support and encouragement to hit these jokers where it hurts. I don't believe these folks will ever treat us like they want us to treat them."

"Do we want them to treat us like they want us to treat them? I don't think so. We all would be in bad shape. This country would no longer be the country it is today."

"I don't want my country to be the same as it is today. Change is the reason I want to kick some of these white butts. I'm fed up with your country's bull. I have hated the ways we have been treated as long as I can remember. What about you Bud? Fred, Ike?"

"Once we get this paper up and running we will have

something to beat the man over the head with. There is nothing more powerful to shape public opinions with than a news paper. You guys remember one thing, the paper and the rest of the news media were the tools we used to get what we got thus far."

"That ain't much."

Some of the citizens had gotten a brief peep at what they thought was the pot of gold at the end of their rainbow. Members of the older crowd began to become impatient because they were coming to the end of their life's highways.

"Guess what I found?"

"We have no idea what you are talking about Ike. It's about time you did something useful for your people. Now come on and let us in on what's making you so worked up."

"You know I once work for the Ramons who is part owner of the county news. I happened to mention us wanting a press and he showed me their old equipment they had stored in their junk room. There in front of my eyes was all the tools we need to get started with. The boy explained each section to me and told me that he would show us how to work them.'

'That's what I wanted to hear. Get with the young man and find out when we can discuss price and times for our training and what he'll charge extra for his teaching."

"I'll have that information the first thing in the morning. I'll see you newsmen in the morning."

The men of the press had not heard from Washington in a week or so and was getting a bit concerned. They didn't want to make commitments that they could not be true to. They needed to think that the train was on the tracks and running on time.

"How do you men feel now that you know all about turning on a printing press? There ain't a one of you who could set type and make sure you spelled your names correctly. Who will be the proofreaders and spell checkers?"

"Au, come on Buck! What do you think was the reasons

we sent you off to college for? Do you have any idea how much pressure we went through every time you had a test? Huh?"

"I'll bet you guys were sitting up all night worrying about my mid-terms. Yes sir, I can see you now, Ike, walking around in the middle of the night praying for me to pass the grades. Yes sir, I know you men were praying the prayers that got me through."

"I'll call our great news man in the afternoon to tell him to start packing for home. His news machine has been moved and ready to be set up in a building of his choice. I'm sure he'll want to rent one of these unused car garages that is being used for nothing more than to store trash in."

"Tell him that the next move is on him. I have been busting my back trying to make a hero out of him. He better show some appreciations for what I am making him into."

"Did you hear what Marshall just said men? This boy is taking all the credit for the work that we are doing."

"I wouldn't pay too much attention to what our great Mr. Marshall says. He is handy to have around at times. But, we will have to keep him tied up most of the time."

The men had gone all out to get things ready to get under way before cold weather set in. They wanted to be up and running full speed ahead before winter.

CHAPTER THIRTEEN
FINANCE

The success party had to be put off until the high-class news men had the monies needed to get the paper machine on line. They had the hardware and the location all in place, but the cash had run out. This was the time for Buck to get on his soap box and preach about something other than where we go in the here-and-after.

"Men, we will have to come up with the cash needed that will buy the paper, ink, and license to get under way. We can't expect to turn a profit for the first month or two. We will need to pay electric and gas bills. The phone will have to be installed, plus we need business cards too."

"What about the station wagon notes and gas? I'll drive it but I don't have the money to run it."

"Those are the things I'll be asking the community citizens to help us with. I will convince our people of what they have to gain from what we are doing. They will be reapers of the biggest gains from this giant mission we have taken on."

"Marshall! Marshall! We know you ain't good for offering cash for this missions, but you are a good driver as long as you are driving somebody's else' rigs. We will let you know what your job will be. So, set down and close that yap of yours."

"What are you gonna contribute Ike? You can barely write your name."

"Who do you think found the equipment to get us started with? Huh? Did you crawl around in a packed rat-infested garage on your hands and knees probing for nuts and bolts?"

"Listen up you two combatants. Save that energy for the fight ahead. We gonna need all the muscles you got for the job ahead. Now, we have everything we need to get rolling except the work assignments. Marshall we know what your responsibilities will be, that is, your firsthand job will be. Let's get to you Ike. Why don't you work with Washington in the printing room? How do that sound to ya?"

"It sounds good to me. After all I did find the equipment."

"Fred will be assigned the job of delivering the leaflets to every door in these United States. You can hire a few young boys to hang the things on our citizens doors. They will gladly do the footwork for you for chump change. Do you get that Fred?"

"I'll be able to do that in no time. I'll need more work than that."

"I'm just getting started. Marshall, You will get ads from the local one-owner businesses like barber shops, beauty shops, funeral homes, and on down the list to yard sales. Can you see your way to doing a good job at them simple doings?"

"Nothing but a piece of cake. The businesses will be breaking down my door to get signed up. I won't have to leave the office."

"That's the way they should be doing, but! Your people might have to be nudged a bit once in a while even though it is in their best interest. You know us. We are starting from zero. What about you Fred?"

"You name it and I'm on the job. I can do all these little jobs and have plenty time left to goof off. I'm good at what I do."

"That's the right attitude to have. Your name will be Mule

from here on. How do you like that for a name?" Did you men hear that?"

"He even looks like a mule in the face. See that long head and the big mouth?"

"Okay, okay. Now, who else we need to assign a job to. What do you men think?"

"There is one you skipped over. Let's see what you and Washington got lined up for that over-educated big mouth."

"Give me a minute to think, Marshall. I'm trying to think what job needs doing and then I might be able to figure out which of you will be assigned. Maybe I can let two or more of you share the extra work, such as housekeeping and so on."

"Go on Marshall we'll let you have the first shot at this one."

"Thanks, Ike, Let's see now who has this boy forgotten. He was given the description of being over educated, lazy, greedy and selfish. Now let's see who fits that description in our little crew here. I think I got it boys!"

"Take your time, Fred. That is a hard one to nail down, Take a careful look about this room and see if he is in here with us. Take your time buddy."

"Thanks Marshall. I think this slick-headed scamp is standing right there next to you Ike. Buck is the only one of us who fits the description."

"Alright men, you've had your little laugh. I did not leave me out. My job will be the hardest of all. I know I don't have to tell y'all what that jobs is. All of you being dumb, lazy, cheaters and downright slugs will make the job of getting a fair days work out of you almost impossible. My job is to keep you stinkers awake and doing your fair share of work. Is there one of you who wants this job?"

The crew was busier for the next few days than a cat trying to cover his mess on a hot tin roof. The work promised such gigantic rewards until these men had to be told when to stop work. By the time Washington resignation letter had expired the new press was ready to roll. He was on his way home to a promising career among his southern kind.

The paper had to have a name to be registered and made legal. The men had to come up with an ear-catching name. They wanted a name that would say it all with one or two words.

"Let's get this name ironed out so we'll know what to call this mighty voice of the black people's. I have some suggestions and so do the rest of us. What is your suggestions since you are the experienced member of this cluster?"

"I have two or three good sounding names, Buck. Let me get them for you. The first is Black Voice News. How do that sound to y'all?"

"Let us turn that over in our heads a minute or two. What else do you have?"

"The Negro Experiences in Print, Or The Voices of the Common Folks. The one I like best is "The People's Press. Now which do you all like and what have you got to share?"

"Don't we want people to know the paper is a Negro publication? If we name it the People Press how would our folks know to buy it, especially those who live far away from here."

"You have a point Fred. What's on your mind?"

"I think that black, colored, or Negro should be part of the title of the paper. This way our people will know what to expect the paper to print."

"You have a very good point there, partner. Is there any other suggestions floating around in you men's knotty heads?"

"Blackamoor News. How do that sound to you men?"

"Blackamoor? What do that mean in English?"

"It means black person, or black people. At least the word black is right in there and people will be wanting to know more about that name and buy the paper to check it out. We don't want to run anybody away because of a racist name. It would be a shame if we let our cousins turn us into the same kind of critters that we are trying to root out from among us. This news paper will be an educational tool for all of us. We don't want to start a fight with Fred's cousins."

"We can always change the name if we think of a better name somewhere down the road. Do anybody have any objections to us using this name?'

"Let's go with that, Buck. What's in a name anyway?"

"You got it Marshall. Okay men, let's go for it. I'll have some card printed up for each of us and I'll stop by the county building and see what else we have to do. Okay men, let's get to planning our paper's future."

The first edition of the paper was thin as a dime. But the men celebrated until the wee hours of the morning. They were on their way to a new way of telling the American story. There were other voices added to the American definition of what it was about and to whom.

Most of the local businesses and churches didn't have to be advertised because they were already known by everybody within the three-county area and beyond. The paper had to tie into a bigger mission, and the big-shots knew that mission was-local gossip. The second needed news was the church schedules and the programs that were offered to the community of church going citizens. The reporters started to pay close attention to what people were glad and angry about. They picked up on long held likes and dislikes. These folks loved to hear lowdown news on their neighbors

"Bud, you better get over to the Knocks and get the story straight about Sunday. It's out that John went crazy as a road lizard and ran his whole family off into the woods."

"Yeah Buck. I had planned to drop over this evening. I won't go to the house. I know better than that. I'll stop by the sheriff's first and see what he has on that fool. After that I'll have a talk with that old gossiping Lula May. She knows everything that goes on between husbands and wives"

"You know that family has been the main grapevine of

black news forever. They were the eyes and ears of Red Rock community since day one."

"You know men, it just might be to our advantage to hang around these out-of-the-way places and get some good juicy news. While you are over there try to find us a good source to gather this kind of news. We want to be the main black entertaining media in the state."

"I got you Buck. It will save us a lot of driving time to meddle in their business, Let's let them sing their own songs. You know how much people love to be heard. I'll let them know that we are their voices and they can express themselves through this here Blackamoor News."

The men were seeing something that had not been clear on their radar screen before. They were waking up to what their readers were really interested in reading about. They would have to enlighten their people about the real issues by piggybacking the real stuff on the gossip columns.

"Buck, there is something going on at the Rogers home. I saw the doctor's station wagon parked there when I drove pass."

"Then why didn't you stop and see if there was anything that we could do?'

"You know how awkward I am around them high-class and uppity Negroes. I'm more comfortable mingling with high-class Whites than I am associating with them Rogers."

"Let me get over there and see if there is anything we can do. That is if there is anything wrong. The doctor might have come out to see one of his white patients and decided to stop at the Rogers to get a dozen eggs, or something."

"Well, that might be true. I'll hold down the fort until you get back. I show hope everything is alright over there even if they are stuff-shirts."

"Boy, you better get used to dealing with educated people if you want us to become world wide like we plan to. You are gonna have to learn to speak real English instead of the ghetto language you now speak. We are gonna start to educate ourselves,"

"Buck, you are already educated. That's why I told you to drag your sorry butt over there."

"That will make educating you nappy heads much less embarrassing. We can get the job done right here if you thick-skull news paper men haven't forgot how to listen, like I sometimes think you have."

The Rogers had a real problem with their oldest daughter. It was the kind of news that the Blackamoor would have to be careful with. This kind of news could bring down everlasting troubles on the whole community of Little Rock. Their daughter was in heap big trouble.

"We both don't have to go in, Bud. Pull over there on the grass out of the way and I can check this out in a few minutes. I'll ask them if there is any trouble that they need help with.'

"Hi Marge! Is your daddy here?"

"Yes sir, Mr. Smith. Come on in and I'll get him for you."

"Who is that Marge?"

"It's Mr. Buck Smith, Daddy."

"Offer him a seat and tell him I'll be right out."

"I heard, Marge. Thanks baby."

"Evening Mr. Smith! How is all with you and family?"

"We are blessed. We were wondering if all was well with you and your family?"

'

"You know all things happen for a reason. God knows what he is doing. We will just have to trust in the Lord. Ain't that what you teach?"

"That's one way of seeing things. You know He does work in strange ways from what we know. He works through the people who are part of the human race to get his work done. He might reach out through your relatives, friends and neighbors. We have to be alert to what messages He is trying to send us."

"I see what you are saying. I hope God is on our side because our oldest daughter is pretty sick right now. We have done all that we know how to do and have nothing left to do but pray. She tried to abort her unborn child but things went wrong. The dead child is still inside her. The doctor is trying to get her to pass the child. Thanks anyway for your offer to help."

Buck saw that there was absolutely nothing that he and his crew could do but stand with the family and trust in the almighty."

This was an example of the kind of news that the Blackamoor News made sure it left to the gossiping grapevine to spread. Buck could feel the vibrations of emotions that will be running through members of two families for years to come. The victims of this kind of trouble did not need to be exposed to every wagging tongue within the three-church communities. They had enough troubles without entertaining every supper table in the south.

"If there is anything that you need, let me know. Rachel might cook up you a good meal tomorrow, if that's alright with you."

"I know the wife would be glad she did. The old woman is so tired until she goes to sleep when she is cooking. Thanks a bunch Mr. Smith. May God bless you."

Food was the first offer made to people who were having problems in the home. This cooking business required many hours of hard work, in other words it was an all-day job for a healthy woman, or man. The extra company and the long hours of wakefulness didn't help either.

It was the following day that the girl breathed her last breath of air. She had suffered enough and gave up the ghost. It was believed that she might have stood a better chance of living a long life if the doctor had done for her the same quality service he had done for his white patients. This lack of commitment to colored patients became a battle cry in the Blackamoor News. This kind of information was necessary until there came the time when this kind of shabby services were no longer the order of business.

"Take a good look at the editorial page and tell me what you men would add or subtract from it. I think this will be something we all can take some responsibility for. We will not accept this kind of treatment from the people whom we pay our hard earned money to for their services. We will demand the same level of care as their mother would get."

"Boy, this hits the nail on the head. We all know this is the case, too."

"What's is your take on the issue Fred?"

"Can we prove that he fell short in his duties to the poor child?"

"It is common knowledge around here of what kind of medical treatment we get. Let them prove that this is not the case. If they put up a fuss then they will have to offer some kind of explanations to the charges."

"I think this kind of news is long overdue. We should have done this same thing back when old lady Emma died without her being visited but once. The doctor was playing golf, or something, when he was needed by her bedside. I even knew that something was wrong."

"Marshal we didn't have what we have now to fight this kind of practice with. We have a news paper today. You will be surprised how many Whites read this paper. These housekeepers make sure their boss ladies have a copy of every issue. The Whites are our biggest readers. They are most likely to know how to read too."

"Then you are saying that this is our opportunity to get at the truth of our professionals and how their attitudes toward us determine how we are served here in our own country."

"You are on the right tracks now boy. Look at it like this, we know what is, but to get at it, we need some way to expose it. Now let's get to work. Bud, let's git down to see the doctor and make sure he is aware of what our attack will be about. I think he should know what the compliant is about. He is our horse on which we will start our war against this kind of crap."

These two cousins slid into town on a Monday when there would be peace and quite. They would have a bit of privacy in which to question the old doctor.

"Morning Doctor! I see your office is empty this morning."

"What can I do for you men?"

"As you know, we are the owners of the Blackamoor News. We would appreciate it if you could see your way clear to answer a few personal questions for us."

"I assume your questions will be about the young lady whose life I could not save. I believe I did all that was expected of me."

"You just stated the heart of our investigation Doctor. We don't believe that you did all that would have been expected of you if the young lady had been White."

"What make you men think that?"

"We don't believe you are that dumb, or think we are that crazy. I don't believe you could expect us to believe you would have done the same thing if the child was your niece. Do you want us to believe you did your best?"

"You boys don't know the first thing about practicing medicine. I stood by the child until she departed this life. Now what more do you expect a doctor to do. Doctors are men, not gods,"

"Doctor, are you saying that you might have done that exact same quality of work if the child had been your sister's daughter? Do you expect us to believe that?"

"Why don't ya?"

"There is one fact you can look forward to and that is we are gonna undress you and the way you do your doctoring on people of the Negro race. We want to hear how you are going to explain that to your house boys and girls. We Coloreds have to depend on you, we think, for our doctoring needs."

"Have you boys done up and gone crazy? Do y'all know I'm not obligated to explain a cottoning picking thing to the lacks of you boys. Now I think you boys have overstayed your welcome."

The doctor's reactions were mild compared to what the men

had expected. They had taken a few extra dollars just in case they were charged with breaking some law, written or unwritten, or some other no, nos.

"Let's get back to the office, partner. This should sell a few extra copies of our news letter. It's time we teach our big men that we ain't crazy after all. I want the good man to have to face his hired help with a justifying answers to unasked questions."

"I think you got his attention pretty good. I can't believe he is finished with us though. He was so surprised when we put him on the spot until he was not prepared for defending himself. He never thought that he ever would need defense from the likes of us."

"Getting his attention was my point. There is a bunch of his buddies who will be checking their ways of doing business with their colored customers and employees. The most important eyes that we want to open are those of their hired help. You see where we want to go with the doctor?"

The Blackamoor News went to town on the perceived difference in the levels of services that the different ethnic groups received. The news asked the service users to check the quality of the service and the price charged for the services. They were told to compare what they find to what was obvious of a lower quality of service and at a higher cost than the White's got.

Buck and the pilgrims held their positions until the dirt had settled in the grave of the unfortunate. They didn't want to hitch their messages to emotions only. There had to be some changing made based on sound thinking. Changes that would make it better for all Americans citizens. Buck and staff waited until the community calmed down.

A few of the smart old white and black citizens were beginning to ask questions of each other. They could see the smoking guns being fired at the business-as-usual ways of wheeling and dealing between the races. This, the men thought, was the encouraging signs telling them that they were on target.

The month after the funeral of the young lady was when the preacher thought it was time to mention something relating to the girl's treatment by the doctor. The pastor was considered to be the voice of the church community, except that news printed by the Blackamoor News. They often took different approaches to addressing the hot social issues.

The article is asking the main questions relative to what quality of service can we expect from our professional servants, Would the medical community of workers be expected to show the same degree of professionalism and dedication to the Blacks as that offered to the Whites?

The pastor preached on the Biblical saying that the least of God's children will be the most. He was asking his congregation to keep the faith and let God do his work. God had his time set and justice would be done in due time. His solution to the social problems didn't set good with all his members. This was especially true for the young who had the most to gain from positive social changes. The old critters didn't have the talent nor the energy to take the advantage of what changes were expected to come from the pioneers' hoped-for successes.

A few of the old generations were beginning to have doubts when it came to depending on a religious solution to solving their social problems. These were considered dangerous thoughts to be evolving in their heads. Most of the doubters had sense enough to keep these nonconforming notions to themselves.

CHAPTER FOURTEEN
CHANGING FOCUSES

The Blackamoor News carried every sliver of negative news created from the lopsided relations existing between the races. The paper was starting to have customers in cities as far north as St, Louise. This was what the big newsmen were waiting for. They hired several young men to work after school stuffing the large envelopes to mail, or deliver to neighborhood drug stores. They were big news carriers when it came to beating up on the way Whites did business with their fellow citizens of color.

"If we continue to get new orders for our news like we have for the past year we'll have to open branch offices in other communities."

"I don't think so, Fred. It will be much cheaper and profitable to open distribution points and ship bundles of our news to those points. Those northern publishers gather news from their city and send it to us here in the deep south. Now we have the chance to send news about what's happening in our neck of the woods to the north."

"I'll have to give ourselves a big pat on the back for what we have accomplished so far. We are making money and doing our people some good all at the same time. We are making a few pennies without somebody dying or going to jail. Now that's a change from what used to be,"

"What do you think about us hiring my cousin to look for drop-off points and give him a percent of the profits?"

"Sounds good to me. What about you Ike, and you Marshal?"

They all agreed with Buck as usual. The men felt lucky to have Buck in the drivers seat. The man thought about little else outside the running of the paper. He was a good man to have at the helm of the Blackamoor News Paper.

The great newsmen had their hands full just publishing the local gossip and the wrongs done by their white cousins. The people who made their living either working for others, or hired themselves out to work for others were often the headlines in the news. These hired hands needed a voice through which to address their problems. The Blackamoor News was their voices in the wilderness.

"Buck, you and your crew have almost run our nearest country store out of business. I'm having a hard time figuring if this is a good thing or is it a bad thing. We have to drive to the nearest store now instead of walking."

"I understand what you are saying Mrs. Jones. We knew that it was gonna be this way for a spell. We are really surprised that we haven't run into more of this kind of hardships. The only reason we haven't is due to many of our people realizing that this should have never been in the first place. Our printing the news is helping to make a gentler transition than it would have been without this paper. What do you think Mr. Jones?"

"I'm not saying that we should give up on what we are doing. No, that's not the case a tall. We were talking yesterday about maybe using a softer glove on the hand when we punch these rascals in the nose. That's all."

"We have gone over this a hundred times and haven't figured out any way to do what we are doing without somebody getting their butts kicked. Do you have any ideas that might work a little better? We are open to considering new ideas."

"I will give it some thought. I appreciate you giving us, across the way here, a chance to partake."

"The doors to the Blackamoor News are always open to our people. You are welcome to come back at any time. We are your ears, eyes and arms in this fight to make life the best for all. We even welcome our white cousins to share what they think would work."

I would appreciate it if you would address a few of the hardships that we are beginning to experience."

"I'll get right on it. You will read something to that effect in our next issue. You won't mind it if your name gets caught up in the article, would you?"

"None at all. I would not object to y'all putting my picture in the paper. No sir. None a tall'"

"Thanks Mrs. Jones. Can I take a picture of you right now?"

"Heavens no. Just look at my hair. I'll bring you a picture later today. I have pictures that make me look more like myself."

Buck saw how easy it was to get people involved in contributing to making their lives better. They just needed to be shown a way to get involved without risking too much. Buck saw where he might be able to reward the citizens for the parts they played. These citizens were nearly totally dependent on the people on the other side of the racial line for their daily qualities of existences.

"How do you men like the article there about Mrs. Jones?"

"My god! That old hen hasn't stopped cackling since you made a famous woman out of her."

"That is a good thing. Can any of you think of a better way to advertise our paper and to get the input from our readers? This is one of the best ways to get our readers' noses in the paper."

The citizens from both sides of the social divide began depending more and more on the Blackamoor News for their social information. The gossip grapevine was still one of the most entertaining source of local information. The grapevine was one source of information where one did not have to tell the truth.

Actually, the gossipers were not interesting in the absolute and whole truth. They would sometimes be searching for ways and means to make themselves feel less of failures than would have been possible without some dirty news about others. There was lots of dirt to be told on one's neighbors.

"Hey Buck! I don't see the news about Joyce and Major. Now that is news worth printing. The woman just jumped up and ran off with that Wilson boy. Can you think of anything lower than that" She put herself lower than a snake's belly."

"Hog Head! Hog head! You don't know that for sure. Where did you get your information from?"

"It's all over the community. The wife heard it from her cousin. Her cousin lives across the way from Major and Joyce. Major was left with the house and their two children. So that's what is believed at the moment."

"It would be no surprise to anyone if this is true, but we have to print the truth, the whole truth and nothing but the truth. We can't say that about what you just told me. You might hear anything on the grapevine."

"You are half-way right, but you will get the news. Some of the news is too embarrassing to the men and women these things happen to. They are so shamed until they want to crawl in a hole and cover themselves up."

"You are getting the pictures. Do you think we would be doing these people a favor by putting their embarrassing personal business in the streets for everybody's amusement?"

"I see what you are getting at, Buck. I remember when me and Jane were on the brinks of doing something crazy and the word was out that one of us had poisoned the other, and on and on. The members of the church couldn't believe what they saw when we walked into the church the following Sunday. You know, and I know how that works."

"The staff keeps it's eyes and ears tuned to the grapevine all the time. Usually the gossipers are our first alert. But, we don't put private business in print until we know we won't hurt the people further. The suffering people usually are busy trying to right their lives and don't need more frustration than they already have."

The rumors got more life-threatening as the days passed. Some of the news was that the couple were still within the county. Others had it that the couple had departed for places unknown. It was rumored that Major might have caught up with the couple and did away with the poor slobs.

"Morning Major! I'm surprised to see you this early in the week, What can we do for you?"

"I know you have heard about my little problem. You know I'm stuck with my two children and no mother for them."

"Yep. The news is all over the county. So, what can the Blackamoor paper do for you?'

"Want to put an ad in the news about selling out the little property that I have. The few pigs, hogs and the old cow and all the rest of what's there except the land and the house."

"Okay, just give me a minute. Hey Shirley! Would you come and take some notes for us?"

"I've never been in your office before. This is quite a place you have here."

"Thanks for the compliment. We are trying to do us and our people a good service. This is the voice of our neighbors and not some opinions and what have you, coming from Chicago or somewhere else of equal distant from the source. Now, Mr. Major, we are ready when you are."

"I don't want to sound like a whining husband who is about to kill himself. I just want get rid of what I will no longer be able to take care of alone. I really don't have a clue of how I will make ends meet after this."

Mr. Major had a pretty sad tale to share with his fellow citizens. He wanted to get the attention of those who were in his shoes or nearly so. His story was about how a good man can be misused big time. The good husband wanted to place his troubles on the shoulders of his used-to-be wife. She still was his wife on paper.

"Mr. Major, what do you plan to do with your children?"

"Right now my mama is keeping them during the daylight hours. I come by and either spend the night at Mama's with them, or take them home."

"Do you want to advertise for a babysitter or something?"

"No, no. I have a sister in Mobile who wants to help raise them. This way I will have to drive, but not too far, to see the children and make sure they are doing what they are supposed to be doing. I'm sure my sister won't spank them often enough. You know how that be."

Major felt better after getting his side of the story out there in the heads of his life-long known relatives and friends. He didn't trust the grapevine to get his position and plans to the community of his world.

"Would you read the statement and sign it if it's what you want. Or, you can take it home and study it to make sure it says what you intend to say."

"It's comes about as close to what I want to say as is possible to put on paper. Thanks a bunch Buck."

"If you want to change something in the statement call us before five o'clock this afternoon."

"I show will."

This was the kind of stuff good social opinions were made from. Buck and the staff would always be growing as long as they fed the customers' hunger for some credible sinful information on one of their own that would build a positive opinion of themselves. The low-class groups didn't get many opportunities to make themselves feel good about who and what they were. They would hitch a ride on anything going in the direction of a little sunshine in their lives.

The pastor gave the membership enough time to digest

what he decided to preach about of the everyday news. This way he could not be blamed for starting social fires without good reasoning. He would give his followers a good dose of reaping what one sows. He could not go wrong when he made his members responsible for their own troubles. This was his way of letting God, the devil and himself off the hook. The preacher didn't know how close he came to telling the truth.

"Who do you think our pastor's sermon was directed at?"

"Everybody knows what he was telling them. The guilty will never be welcomed back in the neighborhood again without going through a heap of spiritual cleansing. That should teach the rest of us a lesson or two. Yes sir."

"Fred, Fred! Do you really believe that others will learn anything from what trouble these two got themselves into? If you do, you don't have as much sense as we give you credit for having."

"Look Marshall, everybody ain't like you. There might be one or two who will benefit by sermons such as the pastor delivered today."

"What do you make of this kind of putting people down from the pulpit, Bud?"

"I don't try to know more than the preachers about how to serve the people. No sir I don't want that kind of responsibility on my shoulders. What is your take on this kind of going on, Buck? You are always reading your worldly books."

"From what I gather from y'all actions and wishes is man don't care how much evil is in the world, or in his neighborhoods as long as he does not have to be responsible for it and have to pay for it. He tends to get a kick out of others falling into the pits of hell. What do you think Fred?"

"People get a kick out seeing somebody's butt in a pinch as long as it ain't theirs."

"I guess you men are about right. I've read somewhere where other's troubles make their fellow men and women feel blessed and special. The spectators feel lucky to have somebody who will keep the devil busy enough to allow them to continue to sin in a less threatening way."

"What can we do to change this kind of thinking? It show don't seemed to be being a good Christian going around getting relief from our sins by feeling blessed when others are hurting."

CHAPTER FIFTEEN

A NEW MINDSET

The new breed was getting into their late years of the young men generation. They were all pretty much doing bout as well as a blessed people could wish for without wishing for too much. They had been good role models for several generations and felt like if there was a reward waiting for good work done, they were entitled to it. These old boy were living examples that a man could make it without depending too much on others for handouts. These men had sat in judgment on each other since old Jeff was a boy.

"The weather men are predicting a rough winter this year. You boys know we are due for one about now. The cycle is about every ten years."

"Yep, I heard, Ike, Me and Bud will be cutting down a few trees starting tomorrow. Right Bud?"

"If you say so. We haven't cut too much fire wood since Aunt and Uncle crossed over to the great land where there is no need for firewood. Cutting firewood for heating and cooking were our fall jobs back in the day."

"Man, those were the days. Mama would always have something tasty to snack on too. That was why everybody took me and Bud to be brothers. After Bud came to live with us we had it made until we decided to get hitched and have a family of our own."

"Yeah boy, do we miss them days. I think those were the happiest days of our lives. What do you think, Ike?"

"My young days were not the same as y'alls. Me and my mama had it pretty bumpy. Remember when I used to come over in the afternoon just about the time your family would be sitting down at the super table? Those were not accidents, you know."

"We knew. Mama always made enough of everything to have enough for you and Bud. She even looked out for my daddy's old brother, as you know. He was there at our table every day."

"Yes sir, those were the days."

"Do you men realize how many years ago those days were? We are talking about fifty plus years back. Here we are thinking that those were our best years. What did we do wrong?":

"We didn't do anything wrong Fred. We just didn't do too much that was right and would bring us good times. We were too busy keeping our heads above water."

"You put it about right Buck. I think we did pretty good compared to others we know, and knew and have put in the ground."

"I agree with you and with Buck too. We have done pretty good for ourselves under the circumstances. Remember what we had to go through to get where we are today. Little children and the young men and women could always ignore a lot and go on and have a ball. But, we fathers and mothers had to make sure that the young could have their good times. Like Ike said, he and his mother had it a bit different than we did."

"We are here sitting around trying to figure out if we did all that we could have done as adults, brothers, fathers, husbands, citizen and Christians that would justify our being put on this earth. Our children are about all gone from home which gives us time to reflect back on what kind of job did we did to raise them and get them prepared for their lives as responsible men and women."

"I hear Morris isn't doing too good. Have anybody heard anything about his condition since they placed him in the home?"

"No more than what we published in the paper. My son is kind of like I used to be about printing news from the grapevine. He wants to wait until he has some solid facts before he run a story in what he now calls his press."

The ex-boys were either retired or nearing retirement. They spent most of their evenings and leisure time trying to get forgiveness for their life's mistakes. They had gotten to the time when their futures were now. They had to redefine themselves and decide what their new stage of living would be. Most of these young old men and women had no more thought about these future days than they had thought about fatherhood and motherhood when they were having the best times of their lives back in the day. They were beginning to wonder about what were their responsibilities for the kind of men and women they had been and were becoming. Time was getting short for planning a future.

"Ike! What are you and the head of the house planning for this coming weekend?"

"Not much. You know we are keeping our granddaughter now. Dorothy is in the hospital again. She had a flareup. We thought we had the infection under control. But, you know how that is. She has always been hard-headed. She won't follow the doctor's orders."

"Something like that would make a good article to run in the news. 'The importance of following the directions when taking any kind of drugs.' Do you believe drugs can solve our health problems?"

"You might have a good question there Fred. The problems are, we are having a hard time finding men or women who know what drugs are. Black folks just don't go to college to learn how to read and write well enough to understand written instructions. They are more attuned to studying for a job that brings in a regular paycheck. We don't study anything relating to what the effects drugs have on our health."

"Buck, why don't we write an article offering the job to the first qualified man, woman, Black or White that applies."

"Let's give that a try. We should be practicing what we preach anyway. That is our next big change. We are gonna have to be what we are asking the other side of the human subspecies to be."

The sons and daughters who had taken over the publishing of the Blackamoor News Paper had no problems with the new image of what a colored published paper should be. They welcomed the chance to change the black news from nearly totally about the lives of the Blacks to news about all people. Time was changing for all social players.

"Has anybody heard how Morris is doing? Who has been out there to check on the man?"

"I'm ready to go see the old bugger when one of you are. I get a bit jittery around that place. I remember when Mama took me to see Granddaddy. Wow! That place gave me the creeps."

"Ike, You are an old man now. You are getting close to the time when we are gonna have you committed. You are acting a bit weird now days. What do you men think?"

"You are right Buck. I have begun to worry about this boy here lately. Did you see how much he ate at church Sunday? I thought for a minute that he was gonna eat himself to death."

"Listen to who is talking. I don't see how you could see over the top of your plate. Didn't you men see what this boy carried to his truck?"

"Look you two, I thought the two of you were trying to see who could eat the most. I thought you two had a bet going. Neither of you won that contest, if you ask me."

The old boys had nothing better to do on Sundays, or any other day for that matters, but to look for free food. Their wives, the ones who were left, had ceased living in the kitchens a long time back.

'"You going my way soon, Buck.?"

"Yep, just as soon as my crew finish whatever they are shopping for. You know how mamas and daughters do once they have a few extra dollars in their purses."

"I know what you are talking about. I never had to wait for shoppers because I let the women travel by themselves. No sir, I will walk to town before I drive these women folks."

Ike had always been kind of easygoing when it came to dealing with the opposite sex. His patience did not allow him to tolerate other's wasting his time. He didn't have much time left to waste on somebody else after he finished wasting his own.

"Good afternoon, Mr. Nickson!"

"It's gonna be a cold one tonight. The weatherman is predicting one bad storm headed in our direction."

"I heard the same thing. That reminds me of something. Do you need some fire wood cut?"

"I will before the winter gets here. This fall is making me burn up my leftover firewood I had from last winter."

"I'll tell Calvin to come and see you. He thinks that you are all set for the winter. I wanted to ask you a question or two relative to what you did for the Johnson boy yesterday."

"Aw, that was nothing. I would do the same for anybody. I remember my granddad used to tell us about the man who saved his life. If it had not been for the old colored gentleman who lived in the servant's cabin I would not be here today."

"Yeah, you told me that story many times. He did what we all should have done if the need was there."

"Yep, if the old Uncle had not risked his own life, my grandpa would not have lived long enough to daddy my daddy. It is always a God-sent when a neighbor goes an extra distance to do his fellow neighbor a lifesaving deed. That kind of deed is hard to pay back to the one who did you the service. The children and the grands might have to repay what's owed."

"Now back to the community giving you credit for what you

did the other day. That was a great good you did when you didn't have to and nobody would have blamed you. You put your life in great danger when you swan out into the raging river to drag the boy to safety. I would like to tell everybody about it. Do you have any objections?"

"None at all. I'd be thrilled to death to share the experience. It may enlighten others to what God expects us to do for each other. And I'm talking about the each other that has no white or black skins."

"What hit you to make you jump into the creek with all your clothes on except your shoes.?"

"The fact is that I didn't have time to think. Every second was critical. I can hardly remember jumping in the creek. When I came to myself was when me and the boy was on dry land. I had him under my arms when I saw his mother coming running and screaming his name."

"Thanks for letting our paper print this story. The old boys will be happy to read this. You know the men I call the old boys. They won't rest until everybody have read about the good deed that you did. I'll write this up in my own words and let you approve it before I send it to print."

"Thanks a lot young man. You are Buck's grandson, ain't you?"

"Yes sir."

The good God-fearing folks were beginning to realize that all were created by the one God. This change in thinking was a bit hard for some and downright impossible for others to get a handle on. This was as true for one side as it was for the others. But it was a start.

The poor Mississippi country group of elders who were working hard to see if their grass-root ideas was gonna payoff before the gates closed on their worlds. They didn't want the sun to go down on their worlds before they saw the results of the examples of how to make friends which they had given birth to the idea.

Mr. Nickson surprised everybody far and near when he

started to attend the historical black churches. He didn't know too much about what the Bible said about loving other races and so on, but he did remember the verse, "Love ye one another" or something like that. The man had no clues of how to dress for colored churches.

"You men watch what you say now. Here comes our permanent guest. I wonder who invited him to come to our church in the first place."

"Buck you have always said that there was only one God. Therefore there is only one true church."

"Well yes. That is true about there being one God but we have different ways of praising our God. We do believe in freedom of religions and freedom to worship in our own ways. Our different ways of expressing our beliefs don't mean there are many gods."

"Our different ways of worshiping don't prove that there ain't more than one god. Do you believe that man will exist long enough to learn which is which?"

"He hasn't made much progress all the years he has been thinking that he knew. It looks like the more he knows, the less he believes and put into practice."

"Buck! Are you men still trying to settle the age old questions about man and his religions? Man, when are you men gonna wake up. It is what it is and neither of you is gonna change that."

"Good evening Marshall. We all ain't like you. You don't seem to give a hoot one way or the other. Did you ever question your own religious beliefs Marshall?"

"All the time. I just don't see where it makes too much difference which church you go to or which religious belief one practices, it all end the same. I'm gonna ask you two educated men the same question. Do you ever seriously question your religious beliefs?"

"Marshall, you have been listening to old Buck here preach for decades. He has had a problems with our answers to what's what for as long as we have been big enough to think."

"I went to college all them years and found nothing that gave me any hope that the questions will ever have believable answers. If man had the answers there would not be the wars and killing that is done in the name of religions. The only people who don't argue the questions are men like our old buddy here, Marshall. If we all believed like this boy all the churches would serve beer and whiskey right after services."

These old timers had been through the hoops together over a period of decades. Yet, they made the same arguments as they did when they started out on their life's journey together. They were a bit more serious with their answers now because of their short time left.

Buck started to write articles relative to the questions pertaining to how we worship our gods. He did not take sides any more than he could help. He found that being completely objective when addressing this subject was nearly impossible for one who was brought up in a particular church. He had to depend on the opinions from men Like Marshall more and more These men were not bias enough to have opinions for or against any one of the paths to a heaven or hell.

"Daddy, are you positively sure that you want to start publishing your positions on and questions about our churches and what they teach?"

"Yes. I have put it off long enough. Don't you believe my opinions will carry some weight? I believe in the one God too much to be joking about him. If we old-timers don't share what we have experienced all these years we should be punished for withholding evidences. Maybe we old fellows can prevent you young men and women from making the same mistakes that we did,"

"I just wanted to tell you that the young minds have not changed since your days as a young foolish beginner. You will have to use all the wisdom you have in order to get these folks just to set still and listen."

"Don't you forget who raised you. I do have some experience of having to get the young to lend an ear. Remember?"

"Here she goes. I want to see where we can go with educating our people. Our paper is now the most widely read black owned paper in the world. You will get a lot of mail."

"You have hit the nail on the head. My purpose is to get us human beings to asking questions of ourselves. Our religious beliefs may need some updating. You know I think I know that God is real. I don't have a single doubt about that, but how do we know what he, she or it is?"

"I know you have always been slow about accepting what comes out of the mouths of others, especially out of the mouths of the ignorant. You will be heard around the world."

Buck went to bed thinking that maybe his dreams would shed some light on what he was about to jump into in his old age. He didn't believe that the results of his investigations would hurt. If anything they should clear up a lot of confusions about an important world concern.

"Hey! Hey! What in the world have you gone and gotten yourself into this time? You have started something big this time."

"Don't you two worry much about what I have gotten myself into, read on. You will see that you old nuts will be my proof of what I say has some validity to it than what these famous and popular mouths are spewing out."

"What do you think this boy is up to, Ike?"

"Like always, his knotty head is always fill with some hair-brain notions. His crazy thinking was what got this Blackamoor Press to where it is today. The boy is not scared of being seen as a fool."

"Buck has always been that way. Remember he was usually the one who got us into trouble when we were boys. If it wasn't Buck it was you."

"Bull, I was the good one. I took the heat for things that I wouldn't have dreamed of doing. Now that's a fact!"

CHAPTER SIXTEEN
THE SEARCH

"Mr. Buck! What is this I hear about you joining the Catholic Church? Are you switching from your daddy's chosen religion?"

"Don't believe everything you hear, Fred. I thought it would be enlightening to learn something about what other beliefs were about. How else will I ever know whether I'm on the right track or not?"

"I don't know if anybody can be positively sure that their religious denomination is the right one or not. The pastor said in one of his sermons that one has to have faith in whichever way he relates to his chosen god, or gods."

"I'm pretty sure that you are right, but I think it will be a new experience for me and the old lady to reach out to all God's children. I enjoy it when I look upon new faces in the house of God."

"You read in the news about what happened to that poor Ralph Smith's boy?"

"I sure did and my heart reached out for the young man. He is in and out out the cracks all the time. People like him confuses me to the limits. You can't find a nicer man than that young fellow. He will give all he has to help out one or us who he thinks need his help."

"His daddy was the same way, remember? The old Ralph gave his life trying to help that boy that came through here running from the law. He got between the deputy and a stranger. They never proved that the poor stranger was guilty of any wrong doing. Remember?"

"You know I do, because I covered the story in the news. We sold out of copies of the paper every day while the community's emotions were red hot."

"Well the son seems to be traveling the same kind of highway as his daddy did. He seems to be in the wrong places at the wrong times. He is driving his mother nuttier than the fruit cakes that she can make that are so good."

"I think I'll go by and see what Mrs. Smith has to say. She might have something worthwhile to share. We need all the facts that we can get."

"I'll see you later. I've got some peas to pick if I want to get some sleep tonight. You know how the old lady is about her canning."

The early vegetables and fruits were plentiful all over the area for the time of the spring. The women folks were on the men's backs to make hay while the sun was shinning. The winter had been one of the worst that any of the grown folks could recall. But, the Spring came on just as strong as the winter had been. The men were working their behinds off cleaning up behind the bad winter and getting the growing season's work done.

"Bud! Ain't you going to the store later on today?"

"Yes Sis. What do you need?"

"I need several cases of quart jars. I don't have forever to get my early canning done. That cousin of yours is out there questioning everybody who will stop long enough to listen to his babbling."

"Well you know he has been the brains of the community for years. We all still thinks that if something is known, he knows it. I have learned just about all I know from his education, reading and being nosy here in these here woods."

"Yes we know. You could always be found near your big

cousin. You hung around him for more than what he knew too. His mama kept the fires burning in the cooking stove. I know you miss the food more than you miss your kin folks."

"You just may be one hundred percent right on that one. Gosh, I can smell them cookies some times now about the time in the afternoon when the wind is blowing in the right direction."

"You know that ain't the real aroma coming from real cookies. That scent is all in your imagination and wishing for days gone by. I don't want you getting what's real confused with something that is gone forever. Do you hear me, cousin-in-law?"

"I know I get a little crazy at times but I'll try to hang on to good sense a while longer. The time is near when I won't have much use for having good sense."

"Just don't you forget my jars if you want fresh fruits and vegetables this winter."

"Yes ma'am."

Buck had started to look for guests speakers who he thought could add new insight to his church group. His articles in the Blackamoor Press were getting some responses. He tried to welcome any thoughtful messages that a guest had to share. The many churches that he visited offered unlimited opportunities to ask serious question relative to what the creation of man was all about and where he is on his way to. But, they offered no believable answers.

"What did you think of my little speech today, Son?"

"You were hitting the nail square on the head, but I didn't see too many who had a clue of what you were trying to tell them."

"It will take a while for my people to get the points I'm trying to make. Man didn't get to where he is today in a month. By the time man catches on to the lessons of today he'll be right back where he is now. Man is hard-headed. I sometimes think the monster is blessed to be as civilized as he is."

"Don't you ever feel like giving up on your brothers?"

"All the time. But, If I do give up on him, then what?"

"Here comes Marshall. Let's see what he says on this thing about us. Hay Marshall! How low is the hammer hanging today?"

"Howdy men. What big problems are you men solving today?"

"We are working on the biggest and need your help. What do you think man is and where do you think he came from? Now take your time and think about the question hard before you give us your answer. We kind of know what your answer will be. Go ahead and shoot."

"Man came from the same place that all the rest of God's critters did. Man came from his mammy and daddy, where else. Ain't that enough to know?"

"It's no wonder you got kicked out of school. Do you ever wonder why you are here?"

"I sure do; I feel my belly kinking up right now. Let's ride down to Maebell's and get us some of her good chicken. Man, I'm starving."

"Buck, why don't you put Marshall's ideas in the press? I bet we would double our sales."

"No way. We want to help our reader understand the world in which they live. If we use teachers like Marshall, our people will be back living in caves in no time."

"If you did let men like me have something to say we would have more fun while we live. All the other bull don't help us to live better lives. The heck with the whats', the whys and the whens."

"Let's go down to Maebell's and stuff our bellies with her good fried and boiled food."

The upper middle-aged made their second home in or near food joints. You could look at their waist lines and tell what they did most of the time.

Buck felt that his highest calling was to serve his fellow man. He could not sit on his butt and watch his fellow creatures flush themselves down the sewer without trying to lend a helping hand. His problem was how in hell does he accomplish this mission?

Buck had a notion that the great creator had a purpose for every single individual creation of his.

"Marshall! What do you think this cow's destiny was?"

"That's an easy question to answer. That question answers itself when you watch Marshall gobble down chunks of that hamburger. You guys ain't watching that boy."

"Let Marshall answer for himself, will you?"

"Okay Buck. What is your answer to Buck's question?"

"This, what ever it is, was put here to do exactly what it is doing. This thing was meant to be enjoyed by hungry mouths. Do that answer your question Buck?"

"Coming from you? Yes. That is what we expected you would say. Did any of you men think happy-go-lucky here would say anything that showed a little mercy for the cow?"

"Read your Bible if you don't believe me. Even the prophets sacrificed these critters to their gods,"

The cold fall weather was true to the weather man's forecast. The little balls of ice rained down like the angel Gabriel was mad at mankind. The outdoor animals were even caught without their full coats of winter fur. These critter had to become friends in order to huddle together and share their body heat. Even the competing strapping bulls made temporary peace with one another. The human animals had also become housebroken during the whiteouts,

"Buck, it looks like we are in for the winter of the century. What are we old codgers gonna do with all this idle time except worry the old women to death?"

"I'm working on something that we all can take part in? We need to have a few sessions where we can share the lessons we've learned from all them mistakes that you, Fred and Ike made in y'all's lives."

"Ike, are you listening to what our teacher is saying?"

"He is partially right. We made two or three mistakes and a lot of successes. Look at him now. He made umpteen mistakes to our few."

"What in the dickens are you boys saying? We were all in the mistaking business together. Remember?

"We know Buck. But you were more guilty than we were because you knew better. We didn't have sense enough to know better. We just went along with our shrewd leader."

"I want ta be there when you tell the angel at the gate that story. That is if you two even get that far. Y'all will probably be sent directly to hell without the benefit of a trial."

Buck did remember feeling splinters of guilt every time the pack stepped outside the common-sense boundaries. It was many years before he realized that what was tickling his conscious was not the case with the rest of the gang. Buck often remembers his mother's words, "Buck you aught to have known better."

"Buck, we took you to be our leader back in the day, and do to this day. You were the smart one. You see God's gonna hold you responsible for the sins that we committed."

"Ike, if that's the case I'm a gonna. Do you really believe that some of us are responsible for the rest of us? I don't want to believe just because one man might be gifted more than another he is held more accountable than his less gifted brothers."

"It don't matter much what you decide to believe, you were our keeper for all our young lives. You will pay for what you done to Marshall."

"The way you men are blaming me for what you enjoyed so much gives me no way out. I'm hell bound and that's for sure."

"So, now that you understand why we are the way we are, you can buy the beer. Come on let's ride over to the store. As you can see, there is no more beer in that pack."

"We got eyes Marshall."

The lifers hadn't done too much good in their long lives to be proud of. They had begun to question God's reasons for their being here in the first place. They were reminders to each other of the missions that they had been given to carry out. They could not see rational reasons for their being here.

"Come on outta there Ike. You can talk to John some other time. It's cold out here and we need something to warm us up. Grab a bag or two of snacks."

"Calm down you worthless use-to-be men. This beer and wine ain't going nowhere. We have to be nice to the boy here. He hasn't had anybody to talk to all day. So, be friendly to the people who are nice to you."

"Stop your preaching and git your butt out of there"

"This boy's daddy sold me the first wine we ever bought. He would sell to us underage Blacks when he would not sell to the underage Whites. How do you figure that?"

"Ike, you know the answer to that. He didn't give a hoot about us colored boys. There was nothing our daddies could do to him for breaking the law. That was the way it was. Now let me hear you men blame the old white man for our sins. Do y'all believe he sinned by selling us underage boys beer and wines?"

"Will you answer Buck's question Fred?"

"No, the store owner ain't responsible for the sins of colored folks. They have enough sins of their own to give in account of. They might have a different master to serve."

"What about you Marshall?"

"There is no sin in drinking beer and wine. If God didn't want us drinking it he would not have put it where we could get it. Don't we believe in the powers of the gods whom we serve? I know I would never touch something that my god forbids."

"Okay men. We heard our lesson for the day. Mr. Marshall gave us the green light to go on and knock ourselves out."

Thanks Marshall. Now, let's get to doing our god's will."

The illiterate bunch had a ways to go trying to find logical answers to their important questions. They made it their business to share their experiences gained from their journeys down a long road of of life. They were eager to share with anybody who had the time and interest to participate.

CHAPTER SEVENTEEN
THE QUESTIONS

Buck and Bud were slowing down a bit due to aching bones and muscles. But, they were more than ever interesting in answers to the age-old questions of why God made man. They continued to share their concerns with members of the old crowd who were still willing to listen. These men were cruising down the winter side of the mountain of life. A few had made a mess out of the blessings that they were given to make the trip through life an adventure to be enjoyed.

"Bud, how is that old leg of yours this morning?"

"About like always. It won't get any better."

"Come on now, cousin. You just might be able to skip and hop again once I finish preaching to you. Take a look in the Good Book and read what it says about beliefs and faith. Don't you believe in your own article of faith? It has been proven that man has the powers to make himself whole."

"I sometimes have a few doubts here in my waning years. I've always known that you had doubts about everything since we were in our mother's arms."

"That's nothing to worry about, Bud. We all have doubts about what we take for the truth and have no proof of. Remember

Peter in the Bible? Remember how hard of a time Jesus had convincing Peter of who Jesus was? Jesus had a tough time making believers of his followers that he was the son of the living God?"

"Yeah I've heard the stories all my life, as you know. They doubted the words of Christ and they were there to witness the miracles that he performed."

"You see our little slips ain't nothing compared to theirs. Those boys were there to watch the Savor raise the dead and they still had big doubts."

Even though Buck had problems convincing members of his associates, he had a bigger problems convincing himself of what they tried their best to practice and be true to on a daily bases. It was nearly impossible to believe without a shadow of a doubt, without absolute proof what the Bible said. The same events used to prove that there was a divine power looking after man's interest could be used to prove the opposite.

Buck's article in the Blackamoor News continued to be read by hundreds of thousands of interested readers. He had provided good reasons for man to believe in something bigger than himself. But, the older he got, the more questions he had to answer in his own private mind.

"How did you like the sermon today, Herb?"

Herb was one of the oldest members of the church. Herb had spent most of his life in the north working for some steel mill. He returned to Mississippi after his wife passed. They had no children so he had no reason to remain in the north in the cold winters. His wife had been born and raised up there.

"The man hit the nail on the head. He placed man's destiny in man's own hands. I like to believe that we are what we make out of ourselves. which gives man more faith in his own powers."

"Herb, do you really believe that what he said was a hundred percent true?"

"Maybe not a hundred percent true, but enough to give one hopes. Without something to hold on to and believe in, what is left to make this journey we call life worth the troubles. I want to believe that my wife is tucked safely in the bosom of Abraham. I want to believe that we will be together again soon."

"Boy, you give me more faith, Herb. We need something to hang on to. I just wish that we had more evidence to support what we are trying to practice. Herb, I believe there is all the proof we need to not only have faith, but to know beyond a shadow of a doubt. Where this knowledge is, is beyond me at the present time."

"My wife was a strong believer in the scripture. Her faith was where I got my convictions from. She was so into her religion until she lost her fear of death. She met her destiny with a smile."

"These end-of-life experiences kind of help me to hang on to my old fashion religions. I have witnessed the same thing in others who knew that their time on this earth was coming to an end. It was one of my greatest convictions when I saw these kinds of departures from this life. What I'm searching for is that absolute proof of what we are in for once we cross the great divide."

"Me to, Buck. We might have to wait until we cross the great divide before we know what is what for sure. Until them we will have to trust what our instants tell us. Do you see any other way Buck?"

"Not yet Herb. We better dig soon because I have a hunch that time is running out for all mankind, and all the other creations of God's. Have you been reading what our scientific communities are coming up with? It scares the living daylight out of you. Just think about the age of this earth and what they are saying about the likely-hood of our total universe blowing itself to pieces."

"I try to stay away from that kind of reading. I don't read much other than our news and the Bible. Reading your articles and the Bible is scary enough without all this other new information these folk are coming up with.'

"Don't you ever think up reasons to make you wonder?"

"No! Not any more than I have to and then I get down on my knees and ask God for forgiveness for my doubts."

"Herb, you might be doing the right thing, who knows for sure. I wonder about all the other social practices that are totally different from ours. I wonder do these people have the same love for their ways of life as we have for ours. You do know that we are a small percentage of the world's population that believe what we believe, don't you?"

"Yeah, and we might be that small group that is bound for heaven. The Good Book says that the many will be lost. Remember our pastor preaching about the flood? How many were lost compared to the number that was saved. Now what do you make of that?"

"Let's have another round of this good beer. The confusion will clear up after another round or two of Robert's happy juice."

There was stuff people made for such confusions. The fears and doubts seem to disappear little by little as one got dizzier and dizzier from consuming his man-made nerve build-uppers. By the time these old men were ready for bed they had no doubts about anything. They were men in charge.

"Well men, it's long past my bedtime. I'll see you bar flies tomorrow at the same watering hole."

"Night Buck! We'll pick you up tomorrow. You too bud."

These old goats had supper waiting because to go to bed with a belly without food was asking for a bad day in the morning. Going to sleep with nothing but happy juice in their bellies was a no-no. They would be sick for several days. They had to take good care of themselves if they wanted to continue to enjoy what they did on a daily bases. They didn't have much responsibilities except keeping somebody with a job. These boys were good at what their daily behaviors had boiled down to. Their jobs were to keep the young in the know.

Old men with experience with the art of social drinking should have learned how to continue their daily habits in a survivable way. The experienced drunks knew when to fold their chairs and retire to the kitchen and the bedroom. The wise men became booze sippers.

The time of the year had come when these aged devils would have to spend the biggest part of their day inside where it was warm. Their old bones would be screaming loud enough to be heard in the next house. Talking about remedies for what ails you took up most of the conversations among the bench warmers. If it was not a digestion problem, it was a bone problem. It really would be none of these.

"Mr. Buck, how is all with you? Praise the Lord."

"I'm doing about as good as the devil allows me to do. How is the family, Reverend?"

"We are blessed to be here. I thank the Lord for every day we are blessed to rise and shine."

"What can we do for you Reverend?"

I'm on my way to the hospital in Jasper to see Flo. I thought you might want to tag along. You must have heard by now what happened last night to her."

"No sir, I was tied up over at my son's place until late yesterday."

"Well Flo is in pretty bad shape from what I hear."

"What happened?"

"You know how Flo is. She is as good as gold. She is good as gold to everybody. Midge thought Flo was being as good as gold to her man. Thing got out of hands as the tempers flared."

"Keep talking Reverend while I get my hat and coat. Let me tell the wife that we are off to see what we can do for Flo;"

"What happened?"

"Midge decided to give Flo a facial make-over. She waited for Flo on the porch of Ray's place with a jar of potash mix. I hear it was bad."

"I know Midge wasn't that crazy with jealousy."

"We can see for ourselves. Everybody knows how Flo is and has always been. The poor woman is to be admired to have gone through life like she has and still wear a smile. She has been branded since she had a child by that white man."

Flo would never look the same again. The lye had done a job on the poor woman's face. The doctors said that she was lucky that the potash missed her eyes.

"Midge's reasons for doing what she did hangs on insanity. Over what she calls her man? Sam ain't never been worth a sack of dead flies."

The old timers had a hard time looking at the poor girl's face. Flo's face was covered with all kinds of salves and cream. They had no bandages on the burns. The men expressed their sympathies and got out of the room as fast as was polite.

"What do you think should be done to Midge, Buck?"

"Anybody who would do that to anything, much less to a human, should be locked up and the key thrown in the trash can. Flo's life was rough enough as it was without all this. I wonder who is caring for her two children."

"She has that younger sister there. That street walker came back the other day and it appears it was a good thing she did. Do you think Midge will get some time for doing this unspeakable thing to Flo?"

"It' will depend on how the judge feel when he hears the case. You know the justice system cares less about what Blacks do to each other. They will punish according to how they feel about the criminal. The judges hope we all kill ourselves off down to a safe number."

"That kind of justice from our law enforcers has change since we were young, Buck. We get a little more attention from the system now days than we used to."

Midge was not even charged for what she did. There was nobody to file charges and the law gave less than a hoot. The Whites cared about as much about colored justice as the Colored cared about white justice. The two were not concerned the least bit about how the other side treated their own kind.

Buck wanted to ask the preacher for his opinion of what he thought was God's take on such as this. But he thought he would wait until a better time to ask the question. Buck was having more sober thoughts the closer he got to the finish line. He did not fear death as much as a man believing the way he believed should, He thought one who asked too many questions about what everybody knew to be true, should have more fears too.

"What did Flo look like Buck?"

"Man you don't wanna know. She won't be easy on the eyes for the rest of her days."

"It's bad then. I see Midge is still hanging around the joint as usual. She don't seem to be too concerned about what she did."

"Fred, Midge might not realize exactly the degree of harm she has inflicted on the poor woman. If Midge was crazy enough to do something that horrible to Flo, she might be crazy enough to not know what she did. I'm wondering what Flo might do to Midge."

"Flo may be mad enough to do harm. I don't believe I have ever seen the woman upset over anything. She has been a good role model for showing all of us how to be calm under trying conditions. Don't you think the woman has a positive attitude toward bad people including the one who don't cotton to her."

"There were a few ladies, and still is, who didn't trust their menfolk around Flo. She was an eye catcher and that was for sure. I even took a few glances at the lady."

"Forget it Fred. At your age looking is about all that you can do. We do what we are best at, and that is sitting around sipping beer and wines."

The hospital discharged Flo within a time limit that seemed like far too early but that was the hospital for you. The burns had not healed to the point of not being wide open for infections. There were plenty of bugs flying through the neighborhood,

Buck wrote the article for the Blackamoor Press relating to what medical treatment was available for the people of color. It was a well written article which was filled with facts. Buck had used a colored nurse's aid to gather evidence to support his convictions. The old colored midnight working nurse had the opportunities to search unlimited records and watch the existing patients.

"What did you think about that article I wrote Marshall?"

"I think we have reasons to burn the dang thing down and with all then there white folks in it. I don't know how long we are gonna sit back and take this kind of mess. You need to be even harder than you were."

"Marshall, we don't want to start a war now do we?"

"Maybe that will be what it will take. You know how much these good white folks believe in the gun. They have never gotten anything any other way. You know that Buck."

"Marshall, this way of getting our way will have to change some day or man will destroy himself and all God's critters here on earth. We've got guns now that can be loaded on Monday and shoot all week."

"Boy, you have some above-the-clouds ideas. Man having the powers to destroy the earth? Good god. God won't let us do that kind of thing. Even I know that much."

The hospital started trying to do a better job for their step children after a few articles got into the hands of a few of the good Christian board members. They started to change the bed sheets twice a week.

"I see Flo has joined the church and is singing in the choir. She acts like a change woman. The old happy-go-lucky woman is a thing of the past. Maybe it was the will of God's that this ugly thing happened to her. What do you think Buck?"

"I wouldn't go so far as to say God planned such a thing, Fred. I know how it looks to us, but do you really believe what you just said?"

"Buck, I can't think of any other way to view these kinds of happenings. The devil might be involved too. I just don't know."

"We have given high-in-the-sky reasons for all we see taking place in our world. Man might need to have answers to all his possible questions pertaining to the working of his universe. But, wouldn't those kind of answers just lead to more and more complicated questions and answers?"

. "I don't know Buck. You are the great thinker, you tell us."

Where Buck and his bunch went they had these kinds of questions. Time was running out for these men and they were looking for justifications for the hard lives they had been blessed to live. Buck enjoyed these trips into the imaginations of the men and women he had been sharing life with for many years. Yes sir, this was his kind of past-time.

It was that time of the year when their church had their thanksgiving and appreciation for having gathered in the crops. This was the day when everybody sinned through devouring everything in sight. They would eat themselves nearly to death without feeling the least bit guilty. They blamed God for blessing them to the point of having too much to eat. It was thought that anything could be done without sinning if if was done for the right reason. Over eating was done on church property and so that the food didn't go to wast.

"Good afternoon Flo. How have you been doing these days?"

"I'm blessed to be here standing in this very spot. How have you been doing Mr. Buck?"

"It's just what you said. I'm blessed to be standing here talking to a nice young lady. Thanks for being concerned."

"We better get over there and do like the others. They are filling them plates to the limits."

"You go right on over there Flo. I'll have to wait for the old lady. She is creeping around on her walking stick these days. We will wait until the line is shorter."

The sun was right for outdoor eating. It was too cool for flies and gnats to be much of a bother. The greedy Christians were blessed to not have the irritating insects to be bothered with.

"Hey Buck! Ain't you gonna get you some of this good eating?"

"In a minute. I'm waiting for the misses to get back from the outhouse. She likes to fix her own plate. She says I don't have any idea how to fix a good plate of grub."

"She ought to know. She has been putting up with you for a century."

"Feel that chill from old man winter? The old man is sending a warning to all who is smart enough to heed. Do you believe that man can know what is in store for him if he would only take notice of the messages sent by mother nature?"

"Buck, I don't have the time to get into one of your question-and-answer sessions when we have to get rid of all this food. Come on and grab you a dish and concentrate on helping us make the women happy. The women folks will never forgive us if we don't eat all and be seen licking the plates."

"I hadn't thought about this feast like that. You may be right. Let's get to feasting and forget about the lesser crap for now. You and I, Ike, have from now on to talk about the realities of the universe."

Food like what these men were facing didn't come down the tubes every Sunday. They had forever to discuss the nonsense ideas that Buck and his shade-tree apes came up with to pass the time. These food consumers were of the mind on this Sunday that man was the beginning and the ending of reality. They had no good reasons to consider any other destination for man but a full belly and a place to snooze.

Buck watched, listened to and helped the people be the top of the food chain. Man was at his best when he became the master consumer in his world. All the other critters were put here to serve man. Old Buck had a small problem believing that this philosophy was all there was to what man was all about. But, he found it hard to argue his point with these gluttons. Buck watched a few men and women fix a plates to take home to snack on later in the day.

The breeze got cooler as the sun sank lower in the western sky. This cool weather helped the women folks with their cleanup.

The pigs went for their vehicles sooner than they would have if the weather had been more friendly. The hard-working Christian bottom-feeders were not dressed for cold weather. Their ward robes were for work, not for sitting around in the cool breezes talking trash.

"Buck, why don't you write something like, asking this bunch to make sure they give thanks to God for his blessing he is giving to his less favorable creations. They were blessed with a belly full of good grub. This time of the season was the time to celebrate and give thanks."

"What make you think of yourself as being less the favorite of your God's human creation?"

"Well ain't that what most of us think? If that is not the case, why don't we have what God's light colored folks have? Our being his less blessed people is plan for everybody to see."

"I'm not gonna debate this with you Ike. I don't have the answer to such an age-old question. We might never know why things are the way they are. That knowledge might be beyond our ability to comprehend."

"Buck! What's going on with Midge and James? Do they look like they are about to get into a fight?"

"I don't know. I'm going over and get a closer hearing. This might make some good reading. I might be able to use their disagreement teaching material to teach my young readers a lesion or two."

James was getting into Midge's butt for what she had done to Flo. This issue was breaking the couple apart even though the incident was weeks old. James was claiming that Flo's insanely jealous mind was the cause of her doing a terrible thing to another. He had realized how dangerous Midge could be. He was desperately looking for a way to end the relationship and keep his head on his shoulders in the meantime.

Midge made some strong threats and stormed off to the lady's outhouse. The eating slowed down a bit because the eaters didn't trust Midge to do the right thing even on church property. The congregation resumed their feasting after they were sure Midge was not coming back firing a pistol.

"How is things going with you James? Is all gonna be alright?"

"Mr. Buck, you tell me. I'm up to my neck with not knowing what my next move will be best for me to take. What do you see as a way out of this mix?"

"I thought your uncle still lives in New Orleans?"

"Yes sir, he do but it has been a while since I saw him. The old man is getting on in years you know. He is nearly your age."

"Yeah, we grew up nearly together. They lived over in the Casper area. We seldom went to the same church or school. Do you know his phone number?"

"Are you suggestion what I read into this what you are saying?"

"There are times when a man has to do strange thing to get himself out of a position that ain't working and maybe never will. Just something to think about. If I were you I would do some hard thinking this very day."

Buck continued to the men's outhouse so the two would not draw too much one-on-one attention. Buck wanted as little to do with James and Midge as possible while belonging to the same church. Buck grew up with James's father who had met his maker a long time back.

James's daddy had nothing but bad luck. That was the way it looked to the community back in those days. He was the only boy in school who could get into trouble when he was alone. Mack had only one child and that was James. Mack lost James's mother when she was giving birth to James. Buck had no satisfactory explanations for those kinds of blessings no matter what or who was responsible for such.

Nudged by Buck's hints, James decided it was time to see his aging uncle. He left right after the eating contest ended. He had very little to pack for the trip. A pillow case was usually about all that was needed to hold the few pieces of clothing that these middle class colored people had.

The following week after the big hogging out it was time to take another look at what the people were celebrating. Of course they would use eating to celebrate a death in the family. The summer had been wetter than what rain was required to make bountiful crops. The heavy rains tended to wash the fertilizers down the hills into the creeks and rivers. Plus, the farmers were rained in and could not work the cash crops as needed.

The elders didn't have to worry much about being rained in because they were porch sitters, most of the time any way. These old boys had more ears to listen to their tails of what it was like in their yesterdays than was good for the telling of the truth.

The Blackamoor News kept silent about James's disappearance. Buck and other old board members tried their best to not print news that would crank start an emotional reaction that had the potential of getting somebody killed. Buck and fellow porch dwellers were very attuned to their devout neighbors' inclination of not hesitate to do a fellow man harm if it could be honorably justified.

"Buck have you heard from our boy, James, lately?"

"No, but I'm sure he is doing just fine. There come times when a man has to do what is necessary in order to avoid trouble. This action may be to save himself trouble, or to save others. Also it may help the situation if all of us would let the man do what he has to do without us getting ourselves involved over our heads."

"What you are saying is nothing but the absolute truth in this case. I don't know where people like that Midge come from. God must have been taking a nap when she rolled off the assembly line."

"Do you really think it's God's fault that we have her kind of folks among us? I sometimes wonder about what we have right here in front of our faces and how we can come up with excuses for it being the way it is. Sometimes I wonder."

"If what the Bible says is true, what else has the power to create people no matter what they turn out to be?"

"I don't know the answer. I'm rereading the Holy Bible again for the fourth time in search for answers such as the ones you are trying to answer. Take a look around you Ike, and tell yourself what it is you see. Do you see the evidence of God's handy work all around you?"

"Buck, you have been struggling with the questions relating to the existing gods every since we were boys, and you are still at it. Why can't you do like the rest of your fellow men and accept and trust what is known and taught."

"Ike, why do you think there is a high percentage of hypocrites among the supposed to be believers?"

"That question do stumble through my mind once in a while. But, I'll tell you how I deal with them kinds of doubts. I go back to what the Bible says and accept that as the gospel. Then I do like our pastor tell us to do. Fall down on my knees and pray."

"The question remains. Pray to whom, to what and how?"

CHAPTER EIGHTEEN
Changing Minds

Buck was having a rough time thinking about what his life was gonna be like now that his oldest friend had been laid to rest. Buck was with Fred during his last days when there was no hope that he would survive his failing kidneys, In a way it was a relief to see Fred at complete peace again. The man had aged a lot the last year before they knew that the end was near.

"Ike will you pull into the store for a minute. I need something that will make me feel better right now. What about you, old friend?"

"Don't you worry none. I don't think this old truck would pass that beer keg if I wanted it to."

"Fred show didn't look like he gave a diddlysquat about anything more forever. He had never looked better. Do you wonder where the man is right at this minute?"

"You heard the sermon, didn't ya? The old man knew what to say that would make the family and friends feel a lot better."

"I thought he did a good job too. The part of the end of Fred's life that bothers the hell out of me was not his burial but the last year leading up to the end. His last days made me realize why we need something persuasive to believe in, especially in times like he went through. It does not make much difference what it is as long as it brings relief by giving a person some kind of reasonable hope."

"The sermon was about what a soul has to go through before it qualifies for that everlasting peace and happiness. This process, he said, was God's way of making man reap what man sows and at the same time, prepare him for an everlasting life of heavenly bliss."

"I could easily assume from his message that a person is a sinner the moment he is conceived and will have to go through some big changes and suffering before he is allowed to pass through the pearly gates. I might be missing something that he said. What do you think Bud?

"I stopped taking what them folks say to be the total truth a long time ago. Y'all know that."

"That's about the way I'm beginning to believe we all did. I can't see many of the members swallowing what they preach hook line and sinker. Anyway, the old friend of ours didn't have too many there who knew him well enough to care much one way or the other."

"That ain't nothing compared to who will be crying over our old bones If we don't soon follow Fred. You see at our age there is nobody who knows us well enough to feel a loss with our crossing the great river."

"Do we have to die young in order to have a big send away when we give up the ghost? It kind of looks that way. Remember that old white man who they said was way over a hundred years old? He lived alone for the time before any of us could remember. There was hardly anybody at his funeral and even less at his burial. Those who went only went out of curiosity. He had no love ones left to wave good bye to an old slugger of his age."

"You don't have to wonder much now. Just take a good look at us old timers and see who you see coming to our rescue now days. We can name but a few who come to church now. What do you see for us down the road a few years from now?"

Buck and the remaining members of the past started to hang around the Sears and Roebuck store to have more contact to their world. Buck was missing old Fred more than ever even though the man had been gone only a short time. There just was nothing, or nobody, left to take a missing friend's place.

"Buck, how is Rachel doing these days?"

"She is about the same. The doctor don't even know how to treat her. She is okay at times and at other times she has no idea who I am."

"She still speaks to me like she always did. That was not much, as we know. I think she was blaming your friends for your shortcomings."

"There are times when I can hardly stand to look at what once was a great gal. Now all I can see and hear is the shadow of what she used to be. I'm beginning to have sleepless nights which is something that I never had all these years."

"Maybe you and me need to pay more attention to what our religion teaches us. Fred had a stronger faith in the gospel than you and me. He was deep into his religion right up to the end. I could see that he might have had something that you and me are missing. We might need to take another approach to this thing we call our Christian way of life."

"I'll admit one thing that is true about what I'm doing. I'm beginning to pay more attention to our preachers and what the radio ministers say than I once did. Yes sir."

"I see you don't write the same kind of articles you did a few years ago. I thought it was because you were getting too old to think."

"Ike, I still have a hell of a time trying to figure out what this whole thing we called life is about. If you practice your daily habits like you are instructed to, it don't make good sense. I hear little children making more sense than our pastor do. I don't know if I'm crazy or the others are crazy."

"Buck, maybe we are all falling short of knowing what the answers are. I don't even try to answer a question that can't be asked. We are to far into our tomorrows for a different batch of answers to do us much good now. Suppose you learned that there is no god, there is no heaven or hell, there is nothing like we were taught, then what?"

"I don't think that is what I see in my head. You and everybody knows that there can't be nothing. But, if what we think we know is nothing but illusions, then what?"

"Here comes a smart man, let's ask him. Hey, Marshall! How is that back of yours doing you?"

"You see I'm up and about. I get around better than you two old battered hags."

"Buck and I have a problem with our age-old practice of our ways of doing things, and we are at the age now when we want to know if we are doing it right. Do you believe all what we have been told about how the world works?"

"Man, what in the world have you two been drinking? Of course I believe what the good books says. I know Buck has always been a little off center when it came to all of man's doings here on earth. He even questions the whys of everything. I don't believe he has you doubting man and man's creator."

"Marshall, Marshall! You are beating around the bush, like you have been doing all your life. Now, answer the question. Do you believe there is more to man and his beliefs than we know?"

"I can refresh y'all' memories a little. Both of you know I haven't questioned what is since we were boys. You two old geezers know I took what was and made the best of it. I didn't take time to try and rebuild the world. No sir, I made do with what was and I did good, I think."

"You still haven't come close to answering Ike's question. Do you really believe that what man believes is all there is?"

"No I don't believe that we know everything. But, I do think that we know enough to make do. Now tell me what you two hypocrites were getting your nappy heads into."

"We are not condemning all of the way we see and deal with our world. But, is this all there is?"

These old buggers were drifting into the times of their lives when questions such as "Where do we go from here" became the question. They were witnessing and attending too many sick and dying and too many funerals not to ask questions like, Is this all there is?

Rachel lost it all at the fifth Sunday's celebration. She went into convulsions right while the deacon was praying. She had to be taken to the parking lot so the service could continue. She did not regain her right mind while at the church. Buck decided to take Rachel to the hospital before the services were over. He knew that Rachel would not have wanted her church members to see her like she was.

The colored section of the hospital was never the same after Rachel was admitted. Her room had a constant flow of company. The sitting area became a meeting place for members of the biggest Baptist church in the county.

"Mr. Smith, would you come into my office for a minute?"

"Be right there. I don;t want to upset Rachel no more than I have to."

Rachel would get sad and start crying when Buck would leave her. He had to be careful and make her understand that he was not going and never coming back.

"Yes sir Doctor."

"Have a seat Mr. Smith. We have found something that explains your wife's Condition. You understand what a ruptured artery is, don't you?'

"Not completely, Doctor."

"Well your brain is filled with little blood vessels that supply blood to every cell in the brain. There are times when one or more of these tiny vessels will get blocked, for whatever reason, and bust. When this happens the brain cells that these busted vessels supply blood to dies. You follow me so far?"

"I think so."

"When this happen the person will become paralyzed in the area that was controlled by these dead brain cells. Mrs. Smith has had this kind of blood vessel rupture. The chances that she will become her old self again is next to none."

"What do you recommend we do for her doctor?"

"The only thing we can do is to continue to treat her and make her as comfortable as possible and pray. There have been a few who came out of conditions like hers, but those are the exceptions. We can turn this over into the hands of God and pray that he shows her his mercy."

"Thanks Doctor."

Buck had never felt so helpless since he was able to walk and talk. He didn't know how he could face his life's partner with such knowledge in his eyes. He and Rachel had been together so long until one could feel the vibrations of the other.

Buck brought Rachel home the following day. The hospital had a class for people who would have to take care of their loved ones under these kinds of conditions. The classes were about eight hours in length. They gave a train load of literature to study and learn from as you went.

Before long Buck was willing to do, or try just about anything that offered a glimmer of hope for Rachel. He was even letting the magic workers lay a hand on Rachel's head. This was in addition to the special praying groups working the roads of desperation. He made up his mind to commit the rest of his life if necessary to the caring for his long-time wife.

Buck! We are here now. You and the rest of you old worn out biscuit eaters can go about your business and leave Rachel to us."

"You good folks will never know how much I thank y'all for

this what you are doing for Rachel. I know y'all can do things for her that she rather you did than us. Thanks again."

"Out, out, with ya. We women have some housekeeping to do. You men ain't much help with such. Go on and get out of our way."

"Buck, I don't know who these women folk be doing their charity work for. Sometimes I think it's for each other, not for us men."

"I appreciate their help no matter who they are doing it for. They will cook enough food to last me and Rachel until they come again. Y'all should see the house and washing. I don't have to worry about none of it. What a blessing them women are. I thank God for them."

The senior men of the century welcomed any opportunity that offered them benefits without their having to do anything except just be.

"Buck, do you think you have enough energy left to raise a beer to your mouth?"

"Try me"

"You look a little out of it. Come on now old granddad. Let's perk up. You don't have to worry with the females in charge."

"I know you are right, but there is something that we are missing. The doctors are done gone and given up. I just can't buy this kind of giving up. Ike, what do you think about how blessings from God, work?"

"You men know good and well what I think. I believe in what we practice and believe enough to follow the rules. I try to come close to being a good god-fearing man just in case."

"In case of what? In case that what you really believe turns out to be nothing but craziness in your head?"

"I try not to do sinful acts that are unforgivable so that I will have a shot at getting through them there golden gates, just in case."

"That's about the exact same thing that I'm doing. I still

have a problem with doing something, while believing in that something half way. I don't have my heart in it enough to be successful at whatever I half believe in."

Buck was having crazy nightmares about Rachel's suddenly getting all her abilities back, to walk, run and do everything else that she had always done; When he had these flashbacks they would be so real until he would have to jump out of bed and turn on the light to make sure that he had been dreaming. Old Buck would be deep in thoughts about the realities of man and man's existent for days after one of these attacks.

The paper carried news of there being a man from Mobile who could perform magic on people who had health problems. He was extremely good with those who had mental problem too. Buck was not sure which health problem was causing Rachel's disabilities. He sometimes thought there might be both. He didn't know what would or would not work, but he figured it would do no harm if he tried every remedy there was until he ran out of remedies or until he hit pay dirt.

The faith healer was scheduled to be at the church the first Sunday of the next month. Buck made absolutely sure that he was on the list of those who would test the healer's super natural powers. The man's reputation was that he had proven time and again that he had some kind of connection to super powers.

The ladies of the church made sure that Rachel was ready for the day. They would make sure that Rachel's case would be the ultimate test of the faith healers powers to do what they claimed he could do. There were others waiting in the shadows watching what would test the powers of the wishful thinkers' hoped for man from the unknown.

Buck thought he saw a wee bit of light in Rachel's eyes and some improvement in her ability to walk back to the truck. He didn't want to see what was not, so he asked her how did she feel. Her answer came as a surprise.

"How do you feel baby?"

"Fine."

Rachel's answer came without any hesitation at all. This glimmer didn't last lone enough to convince Buck and the others spectators that it was not just their wishful thinking caused them to see something that was not for real.

Buck didn't push Rachel and was happy with any ray of hope he got. He sat her in the cab of the truck where it was warm and out of the wind. He went and got her a plate of her favorite rice and beans.

""Buck you can go on with the boys and relax. You have done your part so let us do ours. We will take over from here."

"You ladies have done more than enough for Rachel and me. I'm sure she appreciate y'all' efforts as much as I do. I'll see you ladies back at the house."

"Well Buck! What do you think about our mighty faith healer?"

"I've had my belly full of jumping to conclusions and being disappointed to death. I will give this one time to settle before I decide if there is hope or not. He said that he would be in our part of the county for a week or two."

"Buck, I don't want you to get any false hopes going. God knows you've had enough of those, but I thought I saw something happening between the healer and Rachel. I would swear I saw something."

"What did you see Marshall?"

"You know me Buck. I believe what I can see and put my hands on. All this far out stuff I leave to you strong believers. We will see how much good the man can do after a few days. You two know I don't really go for the things these preachers and faith healers claim to be able to do, I really don't see much good our doctors and medicine men do for our health either."

"I wish I had other choices, but I don't. What do you men suggest we do under these kinds of conditions?"

"If we had any better ideas you would have known about them from the git-go."

"There is one thing that Rachel and I could depend on and that was. and still is, your help. I have never ate so good in my life. There is a cake or pie on Rachel's kitchen table every day. Man, how can I find something wrong with that. There are times when I have to slap myself away from the idea that Rachel's ailment brought us good luck. Ain't that one horrible thought?"

"No it ain't either. Have you weighed yourself here lately? Huh?"

"No. I'm afraid to get on the scales. I know I'm gaining weight faster than a penned up hog being fed for slaughter."

"Rachel has gain a ton since she had that slight stroke. You two are doing pretty good. Look at how much attention you get from your son and his family now days. I know Rachel likes that."

"It is hard to figure out if what happens to a soul is good or bad. Maybe the old saying that everything happens for the best, or worst, is a true saying. I just wonder."

"Ike, remember when you broke your arm?"

"Yeah, what about it?"

"You didn't want that darn arm to get well. Your folks had to take that sling away from you. Boy, you had us doing all your work. I was the first to realize what you were up to."

"I did kinda of hate it when Daddy made me stop wearing the arm sling and git my butt out there with the rest of you boys and get to work. Until he did what he did, I sure had a good time watching you boys do my work for me."

"Marshall you did the same kind of pretending when you took down with the measles. You even enjoyed staying home from school and church. Your folks darn near had to kill you to get you away from that warm heater, drinking hot tea and eating hot soup."

"That was different Ike. I didn't want to give them bad old hurting measles to my kinfolk and friends."

"Oh sure, you stayed indoors, hugging that warm heater and sucking up all the hot tea and hot chicken soup you could get your dirty hands on. Sure, you were doing the world a favor."

CHAPTER NINETEEN

ACHING BONES

"I see you must have forgot your walking stick, Ike! What happen? You had a miracle come to see you?"

"I couldn't find the darn thing. Just as good though. You see how good I'm walking."

"What do you mean, you couldn't find your stick?"

"Just what I'm telling you. Somebody hid the darn thing. It could have been a ghost or something. There was nobody there but me and Rachel and I know she would never pull such a trick on her old man."

"Well, it will show up sooner or later. You two need each other. One can't do without the other, I don't think."

"Something or somebody didn't think so. That third leg of mine didn't up and walk off by itself. I might be losing it. We are on the top of the hill, you know. There are times when I don't know if I had eaten supper or not."

"I know exactly what you mean."

The remaining members of the younger' pack were at the point in their lives when they could live in their presents and didn't have to think too much about their tomorrows. There had been few times in their lives when they were as contented with what was as they were in their present time. They had their grunts and pain to keep them aware of who and what they were.

"Would you like an orange or strawberry soda, Ike?"

"Whatever you lay hands on first. I can hardly taste the flavors anyway."

"Yes, yes. I get what you are talking about. Do you remember that day we were in town at Smokey's when we heard old man Ralph say the same thing that we are saying and we laughed at the man? We thought his inability to taste was because he had no teeth."

"We were young and silly back then. Now we are old and silly. Is man condemned to a life of stupidity for all his waking days?"

'yep, that's about the way it is. As soon as he learns how to live in one stage of his life, he no longer needs to know what he learned. If he goes around acting like the age that he has gone through, he becomes a fool."

"You know what I think Buck? I don't believe that God intended for us to be smart. If he had we would be. Don't you think so?"

"It seems like that would be the case. How do we know it is not the case? How do we know that it ain't God doings that makes us fools, but our own doings. How do we separate God's part from ours?"

"You once made every attempt you could to address such questions when you wrote for the paper. Now that the paper no longer is, how do we tell what's on our minds?"

"I miss that paper like mad. Back then we did have a voice and could share what we had to share. Look what we have now, nothing. We are right back where we were fifty years ago. We have to get our opinions of ourselves from the descriptions that the white press gives us. We have got to get more black writers on the news team. I know we have one uncle tom down there but we know what kind of situation he is in. What he writes has to be approved by the white editor and staff. He is not allowed to write anything that will upset their white subscribers."

"That sound like something that we old scamps can get into. We can print posters, make telephone calls and preach from the streets and the church. That will be a great thing to do."

"What do you think about us meddling in them white folks' business, Marshall?"

"You know me. I would love something to do instead of sitting around a stove, or on a porch grumbling about what we think is a rotten deal. I'm ready when y'all are."

The old soldiers still wanted to serve on the front line of the social wars. Of course they were in the best position they ever had been in. They had nothing to lose and every thing to gain. Win or lose, Old age has its good side.

"Buck has never looked so healthy since he stole that last chicken. What do you think Bud?"

"Buck ain't the only one who is blowing up like a balloon. I have gained more than Buck has. We are gonna eat ourselves to death if Rachel don't hurry up and get better. You guys ain't too far behind me and Buck. Look at you."

"The faith healer will be at Sunlight Baptist Church this coming Sunday. I'm gonna have Rachel in the front row."

"Buck, you didn't finish telling us what the diagnoses was at the hospital. What did them fake doctors come up with and how they were gonna fix Rachel's mind. Do you want to share that information with us?"

"I don't talk too much about what their opinions are simply because I don't really think they know diddlysquat. I have a Negro College degree and I don't know half of what they be talking about. Do you men know what your doctors be talking about when they tell you what is what?"

"I don't even try to understand what my doctor is trying to tell me. I think that's why he insist on talking to my grand daughter. He kind of ignores me completely. Can you believe him? That shaking old man is nearly as old as Marshall there."

"I've had a long time to deal with this thing and I'm beginning to believe that these jokers don't know half as much as they try to convince us they know."

"Wasn't that you telling us one time how many deaths may be caused by doctor's mistakes?"

"Yeah, I remember reading that years ago. They wrote that in the black news paper. They were under the impression that this was more true for the Blacks than it was for the Whites. This assumption turned out to be false. More Whites died from doctor's mistakes than Blacks. That was because more Whites were treated by their doctors. We still don't go for help until it's nearly too late."

"I'm beginning to believe that might be what's saving us. We do our own doctoring which might not do the job but it beats paying another race to kill us. We can do the job ourselves."

"Buck! I don't care what you call me, but I could swear I saw something in Rachel's eyes that was like the old Rachel we had before her sickness. I swear I saw that flicker of a new life."

"I thought I saw the same thing. I know the man had not touched her at that point. I don't think he saw it either. Of course he wouldn't know the difference anyway. Where did that flash come from?"

Rachel would be nearly back from wherever it was she hung out at on Mondays and be back to her hangout on Tuesday. I'm about ready to believe what the doctors down at the hospital told her and me. But, our pastor tell us to put our trust in the Almighty."

Buck had started reading everything relative to mental health that he could get his hands on. Everybody who knew the man knew he was a hard man to convince when there was absolutely zero evidence to back up what was preached. Buck was a man on the hunt for a belief that a sane man could reason with.

Buck was researching eastern philosophies which gave him a glimmer of hope. These preaching street men didn't appear to have much to lose one way or the other by lying to their followers. Buck thought it might be worth a try to at least take a close look at what was in other parts of the world.

The man was searching for answers to questions that the modern American man was too cultured to ask. Buck had a hard time making sense of the world being like he was taught it was. The Eastern philosophers did have the gumption to ask the questions and attempt to find answers that made some common sense.

"Father Patrich. You know me. I'm Rachel's better half."

"Yes, of course I know who you are. What can I do for you?"

"I want you to tell me the truth. What do you think Rachel and me have to look forward to? Do you believe that you can help her?"

"I don't claim to do the healing. I try to make the sick person see that healing is in their hands. Only they can heal their own sickness. Rachel believes that she is helpless when it comes to helping herself. She thinks her healing has to come from outside of herself. That's the sum total of what I can tell you."

"I hear what you are saying. I have seen what appeared to be miracles coming from your laying hands on the afflicted."

"That happens when I make them believe that I can do miracles with their help."

"Thanks Mr. Patrich. I'll remember that."

"Mr. Buck, remember what the Good Book says about what and who you are and will become."

Buck was having a few problems getting around himself and was worried about what might happen to Rachel if he became disable. He had lived long enough to see the conditions that old age, mixed with a dash or two of self-made disabilities, could do to a family.

"Buck, me and the old lady won't be in church tomorrow.

You might not have gotten the news about my sister-in-law's husband-John."

"What happened to John?"

"I hear he fell through the porch floor and busted up his leg and knee pretty bad. My sister-in-law sho ain't in no shape to lug him around. That man must weighs nearly two hundred and eighty pounds without his shoes on."

"That boy is older than we are by ten years. How old is he?"

"He is eighty-five at least. Yeah, he was chasing girls before we knew the difference between girls and boys. Remember we used to want to be like him?"

"Buck, that was before we knew any better. I'm sure happy we didn't follow his tracks. That man never held a job no longer than his boss learned that he could not be depended on. No sirree, he had no intentions of doing a fair days work for a fair days pay."

"Well, tell him we are hoping for a fast recover for him. We will be there if he needs us, just send word."

"That should make him feel miserable, Have you ever seen him come to anybody to help? But I doubt he would have sense enough to know that you sent an insult to him. He should be told about the time when the storm blew your roof off and everybody was there on the spot, except him.""I want him to know that we all ain't like him. We should be offering our hands to each other now more than ever. We are trying to change the way our people do business with each other. There is nothing that our country can't do that is humanly possible if we stand together as one.

CHAPTER TWENTY
RACE AND HISTORY

The big businesses up north were being put on the spot about their racial policies since the government had gotten in the civil rights business. The minorities who had flown the coop and migrated north to get away from southern discrimination were right in the middle of the work-stoppages. The northerners who pretended to believed in social equality for all were pointing their finger toward the south trying to get the heat off the north. The North wanted to make the world believe that the South was the racist bigots. It was working too, to some degree.

"Buck! Let's go down to the station and watch our northern cousins get their butts kicked. The newspapers said that there were oodles of them coming down to save poor little old us. Ain't that white of them?"

"Yep, that's really thoughtful of our northern cousins. They just might be what we need to get our White, and some Black southern cousins to do right. I'm ready to try just about anything. Wait until I see what Rachel needs before we go. You know I will have to remain at a safe distant from being in danger of getting locked up."

"We'll leave you in the truck near enough for you to see what is going on between our young fools and our old fools. Take pencil and paper enough to record what goes down."

"You don't think these folks of ours are dumb enough to be led into battling each other by a few northern renegades do you?"

"You never can tell. If the papers are publishing the truth, Marshall, you ain't the only hothead out there. There are heaps of bored and nutty citizens just waiting to be given an excuse to go on a get-even crusade."

"I'm ready, let's get moving men. I want to see how you old men look in handcuffs. I got my camera just in case these folks go stone crazy. They have done crazy acts before. We have always been able to drive these people crazy with our constant bellyaching. You men should read some of the stuff I get that is written about the old days and what these monkeys believed and did. They haven't changed much."

"Yeah we know because that has been your mission every since you could read. We had to listen to you talk negatively about race relations and how we Blacks were mistreated so much until we all started wishing we were White."

"You are right Bud. Buck's obsession with the race related news made us think that God had done us a big injustice by bringing us into this world as colored folks."

"Ain't that the truth."

"There is more truth coming at us. We are right where we always were. Nothing is gonna change until we change it. There don't have to be a war between the races to make meaningful changes that will be good for all. We might be the same way if we thought we had to give up something to make social changes in favor of all our ethnic groups."

"If what we are about to do now don't work, what do you educated porch chicken suggest we do next?"

"What do you men think about us stop asking, or more like

begging, for something from the others that they don't have and cannot give us?"

"I believe that if this last movement, led by our religious leaders, fails, we will be doomed forever if we don't think of some other ways to get to the heaven where we think we want to be. We might have to do the exact same thing they had to do to get where they are today. We will have to do what I have always told you boy that we would. That is to kick some butts. Let' prepare for the worst!"

"Marshal, you men think about what we will have if we declare an all-out-war against our neighbors. The United States will be back in the hands of the Indians. The civilization we have built will crumble like a mud house in a thunder storm."

"The Federal boys are beginning to get involved if for no other reason than to protect the first class citizens. They might do us some good by making sure that we don't hurt the others and ourselves."

"The law has always gotten involved but was on the side of the ruling class. I think we might have been better off without the law. You boys remember the riots back in the day. Who got locked up? Who got their heads cracked? You see what can be if the law got involved at the local level?"

"I was not talking about these same folks getting in the act of enforcing the law. You know who the law is here and what they have to do to save their own hides."

"Is it possible for us to imagine the white people asking us to do what we are asking them to do? Can you visualize Mr. Ross, when he was here with us, walking up to my door asking me for his rights to vote?"

"Not in a million years! He would rather run through hell wearing underwear soaked in gasoline than to ask you for his rights to do anything."

"You men see what we need to be planning? I'm too old and too far gone to beg for anything, especially that which is already mine. I will pass what I have learned on to the younger people and stand behind them when they step up to bat. I just wish I knew back yonder when we were young what I know now."

"You have always been ready to take on the big men. The only thing that held you back was you didn't have anybody to walk with you. I don't think it was the time to do what you are suggesting back then. We would have been running for our lives"

"We had a few real men to stand up for their freedoms and rights. You guys know a few and you know how they turned out, too."

Buck thought it might be something the old men could do that would encourage the young men to change how they related to their worlds. He thought he might speak on this revolutionary idea at the upcoming meeting of the N.A.A.C.P. The N.A.A.C.P. Was a voice speaking to the legal side of the racial issues. He knew that the organization could only do so much which he felt would fall for short of what needed to be done.

The rights to vote was not the total answer to the Negro's and the White's race problem. Buck could see that even after gaining access to the voting booth there were unlimited obstacles in the path leading to equality for the Negroes. There were something that would be hard to define that lay in the hearts of the Negroes themselves. Buck often thought forbidden thoughts that related to the Negroes' themselves.

"Ladies and Gentlemen! We have Mr. Buck Smith here to share some thoughts of his with us. As we all know, he is one that has been on the front lines of the fight for our civil rights since before most of us were born. Therefore, we know he has something that we need to hear. He will share his experience with us today. We thank him in advance. Let's give Mr. Smith a big hand!!"

"I thank you good men and women for giving me this opportunity to share something with you. What I have to share with you comes from a many long nights thinking when sleep would not come. There are a few old timers, including me, left who get together once in a while and discuss what might have been, if only... That is the big If. We didn't have the information, or the support back in our days that you have today. We didn't have the Federal boys standing behind us that we have today either."

"Don't you hesitate to ask questions at any time. I will be asking you men and women to look deep within yourselves and search for the answer to the questions I want you to ask yourselves and the men and women sitting next to you.

"The first question is what do you believe would be the case if the shoe was on the other foot? Imagine the Whites being in the same shoes that we are wearing and think about what we might expect the Whites to do?

"The next question is, Do you really think that the Whites have the solutions to your social inequalities? Roll that around in your head for a few seconds. Make sure you know what it is that you are asking the man to do. Does he have the power to make you equal to him as a human being?

'The next big question is, what is it that you want him to do that would bring you up to his social level? I'll slow down and give you time to write down these questions. I think you will need time to ask these questions of yourselves. I'm asking you to give us some feed back either here and now or at a later time.

Now comes the big question that I'm beginning to ask myself. What can we do for ourselves that don't need the input from the outside of us? What can you do habitually that will raise you up to any man's level in your own opinion?

I will try to give you my answers to these same questions that I've had the audacity to ask you. First I don't believe that we would be any more ready to give up an advantage that we have in order to make others' lives better. I don't see many of us who are eager to offer our own a helping hand when it's needed. Do you men understand what I'm saying to you?"

Now comes the heart of the middle ground. I can almost

understand why the other side and the middle groups don't feel that anything would be accomplished by giving up what they have worked so hard for to a bunch of what appears to be nitwits who have no idea of what to do with anything. I'm looking at this thing through what I imagine the Whites see through their eyes. I'm telling it like I see it. Let me back up for a minute and tell you men and women what I saw just last Saturday. Ike was with me when this happened.

"Y'all know Jeff Rayford. We all know that the man is no fool, don't we? ' This man was performing and talking like he was a complete ignoramus. Rayford has two years of college too. That man has proven time and time again that he is twice as smart and learned as the average anybody. So tell me why he thought he needed to display that kind of behavior just to conform to what the other folks work hard to believe. We are gonna have to change what we project out to the world if we want to receive something more than we are getting.

"Yeah, Floyd! Do you have a question?"

"What do you think is a cure for the kind of foolishness like Rayford displayed?"

"I don't know all the answers, but I do believe that we will have to start paying attention to the way we act when we are in the presents of those who treat us with less respect than we think that we deserve. We will have to make some changes in the way we present ourselves to both ourselves and others. You know how we act in the presents of the folks. We even act like fools when among our own. Listen to how we talk to each other. We talk like we have never heard proper English spoken in our lives."

"You got that one right. I have a hard time understanding what my own family is saying sometimes. I can understand the Whites and the proper speaking Blacks better than I can understand my own people. That is a crying shame. Go on, I got ya."

"Men, I'm just telling you what I think is wrong with us. Our biggest problem is not created by the other folks. We are our own social enemies. I have had time to sit and think about this social problem full time since Rachel's stroke. The light in which I see us under ain't pretty. I'm almost at the point where I'm wondering why our leaders don't start demanding better from us. We and our stupidities might be this country's worst hold-backs.

"Question!!

"We are waiting for the question."

"Are you insinuating that we are not only our own enemy but may be doing a great harm to our country. How do you arrive at that?"

"We all know that when the whole team don't pull together and donate their skills and talents the whole team suffers for having the slackers on board, We know what a good coach has to do to have a winning team. Don't we? I can't see this as being any different. Do that shine some light on the message?"

"What I have been able to put together is pointing a finger at us as the problem, not the other guys. When there is a problem in anything it usually comes from a shared cause. No one side is able to cause and maintain a social way of life for all. Now let's get down to business. I'm asking you to start from right here and now to decide what you, as individuals, can do to make this community a better place for all."

"I want our N.A.A.C.P to consider publishing opinions relating to these kinds of changes that we men, and women on both sides, need to address with honesty. What do you men and women think about this little outburst That I puked up? That's all from me today. I could go on forever if somebody didn't raise a finger telling me that I have said enough. It's all your sir."

"Boy, we haven't heard a speech like that one since I've been conducting these kind of town-hall meetings. I can promise Mr. Smith one thing, we will be taking seriously his summations of what he thinks is wrong and can be changed to benefit all. Yes sir, that was what we needed in order to get something rolling toward permanent fixes for our country's racial problems. Mr. Smith, you can rest assured that all you said was recorded and will be addressed. I'm assigning the project to Mr. Williams here. He is one of our best writers about self-defeating habits within our own communities."

Old Buck had never busted loose to that degree in his life. He had always held maybe too much respect for what others thought and had never been as sure as he had become of the truth within his own opinions. He had come a long ways in the last few years.

"Boy you really got going there. Me and Marshal began to think we were gonna have to set you down. You were stepping on some toes and they were not the toes of our great white leaders either. I think you have forgot what you told us a while back. You said one had to be careful who he tells the truth to because the truth could get you killed. Right Marshall?"

"Let the man loose, Ike. I thought he didn't say enough. We know how silly we act when we are dealing with our fellow countrymen. I was always made angry when I saw my daddy and mama having to stoop down to some nut who had less of everything than we did."

"Marshall you are still the same as you were then. The only difference between now and then is, now you have a big group agreeing with you. You were alone in your fanatical thinking back then."

"Okay, Mr. know-it-all. What do you have up your sleeves for our next attack on the wrongs of us and them?"

"Well men, it's like I said in the meeting. We will have to wake up and start being responsible for what, who, where and when we are. The days are coming to an end when we can duck our social responsibilities and be expecting others to do our work for us."

"Go on Mr. Buck. What's on your mind that you can tell us how this big order can be put into practice. We know you have some ideas of how this is to be done."

"You are absolutely right Marshall. We can start with you. We won't let you point your blaming and hating fingers at the other side from here on. We are going to remind you of your possible action toward changing your own habits that will get you further than your jumping on a them. I'm glad you asked the question Mr. Marshall. This goes for the rest of us too. We don't want old hothead here to think that we are picking on his knotty head."

CHAPTER TWENTY-ONE
Wake-Up Call

The old men were beginning to lose faith in their chances to change their world by changing the worlds of others. It was proving to be a huge task trying to get the enemy to stop doing what has worked in his favor all his life. These old boys were beginning to run out of ideas and time. They went in search of a beginning to something that offered some hope for their hoped-for success.

"Are you going out to the hospital this afternoon Ike?"

"I think I'd better or we won't hear the last of it if I don't go. You know how much attention Marshall needs just to feel that we love him."

"I know you are right on target with that one. You won't be able to live here after that boy got back on his feet. My grandson will drive us down about five o'clock this afternoon. He'll drop us off before he goes home from work and pick us up later tonight. You know we won't be able to leave the hospital until they kick us out."

"I'll be ready and waiting for you and whoever else might be going. What do you think we should take him, like something to eat?":

"No, no, nothing to eat. They got him on a strict diet. The old goat will eat whatever you give him. They have to keep a close eye out for what his folks bring him. He even asked for fried chicken. He never did cotton to following orders. We know that better than anybody."

"I once thought he was on the right track. The only reason that more of us didn't follow his lead is because we didn't have the guts to. When others needed a rule broken he was the man to get."

"You are right. We used the boy. We would let him get into the troubles that belonged to us. We just didn't have the guts to do what we thought we needed to do."

Buck and Ike took some ready rolled cigarettes in case he was allowed to smoke. Marshall's free lifestyle way of living was finally catching up with the hard headed old man. His diabetes was out of control. Marshall had put on quit a few pounds in the past ten years or so.

"Wake up you sleepy head. Don't tell me that you don't have anything better to do than to wast precious time sleeping."

"Oh shut up you worn out fleabags. Drag a chair from the other bed there and have a seat and tell me what's going on out there in the world."

"We came in here to learn what you know. You get all the news in here from them gossiping visitors you get all day. Yes, you are the grapevine."

'Buck, how is Rachel coming along? I hear she might be getting better. That's what the church members want to think anyway. They want proof that their prayers work."

"I think she is coming along slowly and maybe I see that because I want to see improvement."

"What's going with you Ike? You are beginning to look your age. I thought I was looking at your daddy when I first opened my eyes, Are you all right?"

"I'm about as all right as it's possible to be at this stage of life. How about you?"

"I don't know much about what my total conditions is. You know these doctors don't seem to know much about nothing. I don't think they would tell me the truth even if they knew the whole truth."

"Listen men, I really don't believe they know how to cure what's ails ya. Look at Rachel's condition. She has been the same for a good while without showing much improvement. We have given up on the medical doctors and are beginning to depend more on the spiritual healers."

"Marshall, When did they say that you might be out of here?"

"Maybe by this coming Monday. They are waiting for some test to come back. You know they have to send the specimen a hundred miles to the lab to get the specimen tested."

"Don't you worry too much about the home front. We will see that our middle-aged sons and daughters take care of things at home. You just get plenty of rest and obey the nurses. They will steer you right. Don't pay too much attention to the doctors. The nurses will have you out of here before you know it."

"Thanks men. I need some old fashion common sense advice once in a while. This place will make you sick if you stay here long enough."

These jokers were having to start to trust the same people who they had never trusted to do their best for the little people. Their trust was still limited to a religious covering.

"Ike do you see Marshall getting better? I just don't trust the staff at the hospital doing all they can to make a black man like Marshall get better. Remember they all know what a hater of white folks he is. Now whose hands is he in?"

"I don't know Buck. It makes one think a long time about ways to make the best of what is and stop bucking the system."

"You see poor people attaching themselves to a rich, or powerful man in order to get the kind of help they needs when the needs it. Marshal has never given his person to anybody. Now look at him. He has nobody with authority to defend him. He has ended up with having nobody to give his soul to"

"I use to admire the boy for how he could tell the man off without batting an eye. Now I don't envy the man much at all."

"Ike, that goes to show us that there is no right way and wrong way. One just reaps what one sows. Man makes his own bed to sleep in and to die in."

Marshall decided that the best he could do for all was to make his exit as quietly as possible. He picked the midnight time to cross the big divide. The old boy was put away as quietly as he had lived. The community didn't make much of a fuss. He lived his personal way and tried to let others do the same.

"I thought that Marshall's going home party would be bigger than what I see here. I know he was not a social hero or nothing."

"The man's funeral was a reflection of the life that he lived. You and I know he didn't go too far out of his way to meddle in other people's business. I think his going-away party was exactly what he would have wanted. He was not the kind of man who could appreciate phony displays of bull. You know how he hated hypocrites."

The old men had something else to fill their nearly empty minds. These funeral attendees went because the guest-of-honors was usually sending them messages.

"You are right about that, Buck. He was quick to get a pretender out of his path as soon as he possibly could."

The seniors had another mind-filler to keep them questioning the whys of the structures of all that was. Buck didn't think it would have been a good idea to drag Rachel with him to his old friend's home going. He let his daughter-in-law watch over Rachel until he and Ike did their thing. They had no intentions of letting this celebration go by without a small pledge to send their friend on the road to where ever it was that he was going to.

"Here is to you, Marshall!"

"So long friend!"

"Ike, where do you think that fellow is right at this moment?"

"Probably siting on a bar stool in some hangout. I do believe that he might be right here with us. We simply can't make connections across that big river he has crossed"

"You know Ike, the more I think about this thing call life, the more I believe that nothing ever cease to be. All that has ever been here is still here. If it left for somewhere else, where is that place where it went?"

"Let's have one more toast and maybe we can get back to this land of the survivors."

"Here's to our friend forever. TO MR. Marshall!!"

"I know he would do us the same favor if he was in our shoes. I know, he will never be in our shoes again, or any other shoes as far as we know."

"I better be getting on home, my friend. I'll see you in the morning, that is if the Lord spares me to make it another day."

Buck decided to walk down the road a few hundred feet after he parked his truck. He felt that a breath of cool evening Fall air would do him some good. The Fall air made Buck feel like he was connected to all that had ever been and all that would ever be. He was getting these kinds of crazy notions more and more in his recent days. He didn't dare share his deepest thoughts with Ike, or the other old and young men. He was afraid that they might think he had falling off his cart and bumped his head. These walks in the night air had the effects on him that nothing else had. While on these walks he got the impressions that he might be all there was to be at the present time and in the present place. He usually returned from these journeys into the outer bounds of sanity refreshed and ready for the next hill to climb.

"Howdy you two! How was y'all evening?"

"We had a good time, didn't we Mama?"

Rachel smiled and lowered her eyes. She seemed to be doing

better the past few weeks. So that's what her caretakers wanted to see anyway.

"I think she enjoys your company more than she enjoys mine. I wonder is it something she thinks that I'm doing to prevent her from a full recovery."

"Aw come on Daddy, you can't believe that for one minute. You had to give up your travel plans to make sure that Mama got the best treatment available. No sirree, you did your job."

"Sometimes I wonder if our doing to good of a job ain't doing more harm than good. Rachel has to get tired of somebody always standing by to do every little thing for her that she could easily do for herself."

"Well, I hope you are wrong on that one old man. If you are right about too much care can do harm, we are all guilty. You won't go to hell by yourself. You've had plenty of help caring for the lady of the house."

"Baby, what is your opinion about how we believe in the powers of prayer?"

"I don't know how to answer that kind of a question. Questions like what you asked me make a Christian question the words of God. I'm a bit afraid to tread that line between believing and non-believing the word."

"I know how that feels. You are still too young to be doubting much of anything. I once was too busy following the handed-down rules to pay much attention to which way up was. You will start to see a much bigger God than the one we claim to serve. But, you don't have to mind what your old worn-out daddy might say these days."

"You ain't nearly worn out yet. Daddy you ain't eighty years old yet. The seventies is considered young these days. I work with men and women a lot older than you and Ike and some of them are in better shapes than most of the younger ones. I'm telling ya. I thinks it's how they take care of themselves."

"Believe me, living a sensible life has its good points. I think of Marshall and how he lived his life. He had a lot more free fun than the rest of us. That's what me and Ike arrived at anyway."

Buck went to all the meetings where there was a promise of help for Rachel. He took her with him more and more. He thought that her getting out of the house more would do her good.

"Hey! Hey! Rachel! You are looking cool this here afternoon. How have you been doing these days?"

"I'm doing good, thanks to the Lord."

Everybody who heard Rachel's answer to being asked how she had been doing, could barely believe their ears. The average church member had given up on Rachel ever coming out of the land where she had decided to retreat to. They were believers in the miracles that were recorded in the Bible, but this was not in the Bible. It was harder to believe one's own eyes and ears than it was to believe what was in the Bible

"She will surprise you at times. Y'all heard how she answered your question. I have started to believe that these social workers, doctors and love ones do a sick person more harm than good."

"I know what you mean. We have watched you take Rachel to every place and people that promised some kind of a cure with no apparent results. Now look at what just happened."

These were the things that Rachel would surprise Buck with that gave him hope. He could feel his old girl lurking just below the outside world and waiting for the right time to show herself.

CHAPTER TWENTY-TWO
WHERE BLESSING COME FROM

Buck thought he may be going a bit wacky when he saw and heard things that were not supposed to be. He thought he might have been reading too many of the Eastern beliefs about the nature of what was and it was making him crazy. Even the African's witchcraft began to make some twisted sense to him. Witchcraft is what the American literature called anything that came out of Africa whether it be religion, political or social. Buck was beginning to have less faith in the modern western civilization's ways than he had of the third world's ways of dealing with man's rocky roads through life

"Buck! Ain't you gonna ever give up on whatever it is you are searching for?" Look at all them old books you have collected from every secondhand store in the county. Boy, you are too old to go on believing in Saint Nick."

"I have read enough to disagree with you, Ike. Man knows so little about anything which makes him a life-long learner. Half of your people still don't know that the earth is round. They know absolutely nothing about what the entire universe is. Then you tell me that I want to know too much? Too much about what?"

"It simply looks like you are wasting the few years that you have left searching for something that simply ain't here, or there. That's all I'm trying to tell ya, old friend. You and me are suppose to be relaxing and taking what is and making do with that."

"Ike, man is never too old to learn. Have you ever thought what man was deep down in his soul? The Easterners call this soul the subconscious. It is believed by some that man holds the powers of God in that part of his being and can do anything that he wills himself to do or be. Wouldn't that be a wonderful thing if we knew how to dig down into man's soul and come up with solutions to many of man's problems?"

"I don't know about that. Man may be asking too many questions already about God's business. The preacher spoke on that very same thing Sunday. You heard him. His text was about man knowing too much for his own good. You and Rachel were there."

"Yes, I heard what he said. I also heard the rest of what he said. Do you recall the other part that was contradicting what his text was about. Did you hear it?"

"I think I heard him saying that man was his own worst enemy and man had the powers to save himself, or something to that effect."

"He said that man had the powers to take up his bed and walk. He said that man became what his habits dictated. The whole remainder of his sermon was about what powers God had given man to solve his own problems. Remember what the Bible said that Christ told the people after they were so overwhelm by the things Jesus did? What did Jesus tell them? Do you remember?"

"He said that they could do the same thing that he did, and even greater things if they had the faith."

"Now what do that tell man? Huh? With faith the size of a

mustard seed man could tell a mountain to be gone and it would be gone."

"Since you put it that way, I guess you are right. Man talk one thing and do another. We put our trust in everything but our own selves."

"Now you are getting the picture. Ike, you and I have been bosom buddies for as long as we can remember. We pretty well know each other's thinking. You know I have been doubting man's way of seeing his world every since we started going to Sunday school and listening to what the teacher was trying to make us believe."

"I can hear you now, 'Ike, 'do you think God was watching us when we took a pocket full of Mr. Drew's plums?'"

"Yeah, and you would lie to me. You would tell me that God was far too busy to babysit us. Was that anything to tell a believer?"

"No, not a believer, but to tell you? Yes. You were the boy who made the rest of us ask questions about what we were taught."

"I'm still waiting for an answer that I can believe. The more I think and experience the less I am convinced that what we teach and practice don't prove one thing. You never was much help."

Buck came back from one of his usual night-walks to find Rachel in the kitchen washing dishes. He froze in his tracks to give himself a moment to gather his wits.

"Rachel! Rachel! What do you think you are doing."

"Aw, come on Mr. Smith, what do it look like I'm doing?"

The first thing Buck realized was there was nobody else in the house but Rachel. The thought ran through his head that what he had been seeing in Rachel's actions the past few months was right. He had noticed that the less help Rachel got, the better she got. He took a seat and watched his love one continue with her kitchen work.

"From now on honey, would you please do me a favor and wait until I'm home before you do your work in the kitchen."

"Why should I do that?"

Buck only answer was, "Cause I love ya."

Buck could hardly wait until Sunday so that the whole church could witness Rachel's remarkable progress. He wanted to make sure that the praying congregation received whatever credit they deemed was theirs. There was no doubt that Rachel had been in the prayers of their church members for a long time.

The Reverend lit up like a Christmas tree when Buck told him what Rachel had done. Buck thought the man was gonna have a heart attach right there in his study. Buck was a bit surprised by the man's reactions. He thought that the preacher should have expected this kind of a miracle to occur if he believed in his own preaching.

"Hallelujah! Hallelujah! God has performed a miracle! I told y'all that all we needed to do was to be patient. The Lord may not come when you call him, but he is never late. He works at his own pace. Hallelujah!"

The church gave Rachel and Buck a standing entry. You could hear a rat peeing on cotton it was so quit when the two entered the church. All eyes were on the couple as if the congregation expected the two to sprout wings and fly off into the heavens.

"My text for today has been changed. I had planned to talk about what the Good Book says about the benefits of giving. But, God has seen fit to perform a miracle on one of our own. I believe God did this to show us what he can do if he has a mind to. Do I get an amend?"

"You know something Ike?"

"Not what you are about to tell me, no I don't know."

"I understood the preacher to say that God's only purpose for healing Rachel was to show us his powers. He also said that God causes these things to happen to his people so that he can prove his point. Do you get the notion that there is a little something off dead center about that way of viewing God's work?"

"I don know what's on God's mind, Buck. What do you care what his reasons were as long as Rachel was healed?"

"Ike, let's get down to the nitty gritty. Do you really buy into all what the Bible scholar gave for the reasons Rachel was made whole?"

"Like I told ya, Buck. I don't question God's work. I'm not that bold yet. You have always had enough doubts about the nature of God for you and me both. I don't have to doubt, you do a good enough job for both of us."

"That's another thing. Do you really think that what you and me do here and now makes a different to the God that our pastor were making references to?"

"I can go along with some of what you are saying about the sermons on any Sunday and in any Church. But, I m not gonna try to second guess God."

Buck had never got what he thought was a straight answer to any of his questions relating to the nature of God. People seemed to be more scared of God than they were of the devil.

Rachel was her old self and acted like nothing had ever happen in her head. This didn't make sense to Buck at all in light of the way tradition had it. He had to know where it was that Rachel had gone and stayed until she decided to come back to the human race. There had to be better answers to this riddle of life than what the people were taught by their leaders. The big question was where? Where did one start at to make more sense out of his or her own existence? He went back to his reading of the different societies and the foundations on which they based their shared beliefs about where they came from, why they came and where they had choices of going. A few made a lot more sense than the local preachers did.

Rachel even seemed to be better than she ever was. She had learned something that Buck and his crew were missing. Buck was determined to learn what that something was and the only person who stood a chance of knowing was Rachel herself.

"How did you sleep last night, honey?"

"I don't remember when you came to bed. What time did you crawl into the sack?"

"Oh. About one o'clock. I wanted to finish that new book I bought yesterday. There is something strange going on in this world that we are living in. This man talks about things happening to people that I can be a witness to."

"Mr. Smith, you have always been kind of strange yourself. Maybe that was one of the reasons you were drawn to me."

"Tell me something Miss lady, how do you explain how you bounced back to your old self long after we had given up on every remedy that we could find in the country. Do you have any explanation?"

"No, other than I decided to make myself the way I was before I got disconnected. I didn't want to be afflicted anymore and be a burden on you and others."

"That's all? You simply decided to become your old self? Simple as that?"

"Simple as that. I can't tell you any more than that. If I didn't do it, who, or what would?"

"The how and what is the questions that driving me nuts."

Buck was more confused by Rachel's early morning answer than he was already. He was reading something that happened to others that was similar to what Rachel has said happened to her. He thought he and Ike would see what explanations the Reverend would give for these self-made miracles. That is if he had an explanation at all. Buck had learned that the more religious people were, the less they knew about anything. It appeared to Buck that the devil and the god these folks worshiped were one and the same.

"Ike, you have been knowing me all your life, right?"

"That's about it, Buck."

"Now, did you ever think that I might be a little on the nutty side?"

"Yep, I sure did. You have had the habit of coming up with the nuttiest explanations for all the whys, what, and hows that you could think of. We thought the reason that you went to college was to clear your mind of all the confusions you carried around. But, you are living proof that education don't cure insanity."

"Thanks my oldest friend. You have been a big help. Let's find our pastor and let him straighten you and me out. You know he has four years of divinity schooling in his head."

The two old men saw the preacher's Chevy parked at the church. They were in luck. They thought.

"Buck, why don't you do the questioning. You have a way with words, especially when they are used to question the nature of God."

"I'm not questioning the nature of God, Ike. I'm questioning the nature of man. Man is the animal that can be one thing this minute and a totally different thing the next minute"

"Same thing."

"Good afternoon Reverend! We saw your car and decided to pay you a visit. That is if you have the time."

"Y'all come on in. I thought there might be trouble when I spotted you two men coming to the church this time of the week and day. Come on into my office."

"How is God being to you Reverend?"

"If I prayed for any more than I'm getting I think he would take back some of what he has blessed me with. I believe you folks called that kind of praying for too much as being Greedy."

"I know what you are talking about. Ike and I have a question for you. We have never heard an answer that satisfied our curiosity."

"Go right on with your question. I'm listening with both ears."

"We thought you might shed some light on the so called miracles that we see happening to people once in a while."

"I'm ready, so what can I help you men with?"

"You saw how Rachel made a complete recovery without

outside help. Even you were surprised at how much improvement she made on her own. What, or who, do you credit that to?"

"I credit all man's blessings to God. Now there might be other factors working in there too, but, I feel safer when I credit the good to the Lord and the bad to the other big fellow. I know it gets confusing at times. That is the reason God calls people like me to help his people to understand his works."

"Reverend, do you believe that man can do all these things for himself without the help of other men?"

"It might look that way in some cases, but God is still in charge. You might have one person over here who knows how to do something that the average person don't. That is when God steps in to balance the scales of equality."

"Let me get this right, Reverend. You are saying that some are blessed more than others from the cradle to the grave. Those who are given that extra blessings need less from God than the less fortunate. Do that pretty much sum up what you are saying?"

"That is one way of saying it. Each man will have to answer his own query about the relations he has with his God."

"Thanks Reverend. I think we got it

"Ike, now that you have a clear understanding of the relations between man, the cows in the pastures and so on, you will be a better Christian from here on. You have something to believe in."

"Yeah. We've heard the same story since before the Reverend was born. He went to college to learn what he could have learned sitting on some of these old folks' porches. That boy might have saved his daddy and granddaddy some cash. I could have told him the same thing that he told us. You could preach a better sermon than he can, Buck.?

"Sometimes I wonder."

CHAPTER TWENTY-THREE
SUMMATION

Old Buck and Ike had become the oldest old porch monkeys in the community. They were told by the church folks that they were role-models to be copied. These men beliefs didn't always jibe with the opinions of the Church, or its members. These two had been around long enough to have doubts about many of the traditional explanations for what was.

Neither one of the old geezers could see well enough to drive. They couldn't do much else that required 20/20 vision either. They were glad of their physical limitations during the bad-weather months.

"How was yours and Rachel's night Buck?"

"I didn't get much sleep because Rachel was in pain all night until just before daylight. I must have drank two pots of coffee. What was your night like?"

"I haven't gotten a sound night sleep since the old lady went home to be with the Lord. You know how long that has been. Buck, sometimes I wonder if a long life is a blessing or a curse. The good days that you and me are enjoying are becoming less and less. What do you think old friend?"

"You know, we talk about those of our day who crossed over a long time ago. They didn't live long enough to suffer the pains caused by old age like we are. You have said many times that they were the lucky ones. I'm thinking you are more right now after a night like last night."

"Are you up to a swallow of our good sipping juice? I feel like getting drunk as a skunk."

"I wouldn't go that far. I have a responsibility to perform. But, I'm ready to meet you half way. Let's have that bottle."

"Buck, you and I are the last of the old group that once crawled all over these here woods and fields. Where are they at now Buck? Do you wonder as you wake from a night of troubled sleep?"

"I have started to believe some of the teachings of the eastern philosophies. These people who were here are still here. They have not gone anywhere. They were part of the beginning and will be part of the ending. That is if there was a beginning. If there was a beginning, there will have to be an ending, of which I don't have a handle on."

Buck was beginning to believe that he might have to stop reading these foreign answers to the riddles of life. He was much less a pain in other's butts if he learned to accept what was commonly believed and practiced. If he would conform, he might not be thought of, and sometimes treated like, he was just another fool who was scared of the dark.

"Did you call me honey bunch?"

"Yes, I did. Would you please bring me a glass of water?"

"One full glass of H2O coming up."

"Wait a few minutes until I drank a few swallows. Buck, you are drinking a lot of coffee here lately. You better cut back on your drinking that much caffeine."

"Are you feeling alright young woman?"

"I can't remember when I felt any better than I'm feeling

right this minute. I feel like I could outrun you from here to the creek and back."

"I'm happy to know you are feeling so good. I'll have to give it to you, you are a wonder. Sometimes I can't figure you out."

"I want to remind you that I think you are a wonderful old man. Don't you forget that for as long as you live. Do you hear me?"

"You can bet your bottom dollar on it. The same back at you too."

"I wanted to tell you how much you have meant to me. Now, go on back to your coffee-drinking and reading your books. I'll be seeing you."

"I know you will. You have nowhere to go but here to look at me. Good night lady!"

Rachel didn't bother to answer Buck's good-night bid. She simply turned her face to the wall and closed her eyes for the last time.

Buck didn't realize Rachel has said her last goodbye to him until he went to wake her. He thought that she was sleeping an extra few minutes because she had been pain-free for the first time in a while. He didn't know she had made her exit. Buck felt strange how Rachel had decided to depart this life highway, but he was not too surprised. He came close to celebrating his beloved's home-going.

"Buck, Rachel couldn't have ask for a nicer put-a-way. You did a wonderful job."

"Thanks, old friend. I don't think that you and I will have the same kind of attention when our times are up. I believe that our women were lucky to have had men like us to take care of them in their declining years. Don't you think so?"

"That I do. It might have been nearly impossible for them to do for us what we did for them without lot's of help. It take strength to keep these old barns fit to live in, especially during the winter time."

"What are you planing for yourself these next few months?"

"I have planned absolutely nothing. I didn't want to think about what I knew was coming in on me like a bad cold. You do accept the fact that you and me are there too, don't you?"

"Yes sir. Why do you think I have continued to live right where I have lived all these years. My daughter have tried her upmost to get me to come live with them. What reasons do you think I had for refusing her offer, other than to be near you?"

"I think the same way you do. I might as well spend these last few moments right where I'm at. Getting used to a new home and ways of living would be just the thing we need to finish us off."

Buck had a ton of research to do related to what his dreams were trying to tell him in the last several years. He was still at the church every Sunday. His ears were always alert to information that he heard that helped him to accept the handed-down explanations for the every-day practices done by the believers and the non-believers. These two mental attitudes were beginning to appear as twins.

The old man, and his life-long partner, were at the church every Sunday for reasons other than seeking the hands of the Lord's. They had nowhere else to be except home sitting as porch monkeys. Ike's eyes were getting so bad until Buck had to tell the man what they were looking at.

"Ike, suppose, just suppose I no longer believe in the religious teaching that we have been taught all our lives. What would you have to say behind that?"

"I wouldn't be too surprised. You have been drifting all over the place with your beliefs for the past ten years. You either believe in more than one religion, or you believe in none. I don't know how you could believe in nothing."

"That's the point. I believe too much in an almighty being, but what?' There is a creator. I have no doubts about there being something a lot bigger than any critter that we can wrap our minds around. I'm at the point where I think the only thing wrong with our old fashion religious practices is just this, they are outdated. Our ways of praising our gods are outdated by a long ways. Man has evolved from the primitive cave man days to these modern times. Most of his ways of doing has also been modernized too. The one thing he has not changed is his habits of worshiping an old fashion god. I want to hear what you really, really think about man and his serving his gods. Go on and tell me what's on your mind."

"Buck, I still find it much easier to believe in what was taught to us than to try and change my mind about the whole thing. You see, you have always had the kind of mind that was never satisfied with the here and now. I have to give it to you though, you have come up with food for thought. But, and, that's a big but, what else do I have to give naturalism to what neither of us asked for. I'll have to do like the normal people do. I will stick with what I believe until something bigger and more powerful comes along to prove what I have isn't good enough."

"We haven't found another religion other than what has been around since man first evolved from a grunting animal to an animal that started wondering about his origin. This religious stagnation is due to man's fear of the unknown, in this case, his fear of death. I believe that man has the answers right in his head. Man, in my opinion, knows the total story of how everything, including himself, came to be."

Buck went to bed thinking that his time was running out and he had to make up his mind about what he needed to believe and do to prepare for the next stage of his being. His common sense told him that nothing in the universe ever ceased to be by becoming nothing. Nothing was an impossibility when it came to something becoming nothing. The old man began visiting the burial grounds much too often to not to be thought of as being a bit crazy. At least he could tell the dead what was on his mind without them calling him a nutty old man.

"Listen up all you folks out there! I have some questions for you. Now don't get jacked out of your minds when I ask what might be dumb questions. Now, What is it like over there where you folks are? Huh? Can you show me some signs that you all are still here? If not, then where did you go to? You can give me the answers here, in my dreams or however, but I want to know."

Buck dug deep into the Eastern beliefs in reincarnation. This belief didn't answer all his concerns with the after death thing but it was a better hitching post for his thoughts than the Western beliefs were. It made sense because it solved the problems he had with anything becoming nothing after death. The concept of death as an end to something's existence was not possible according to what man's scientific studies had told him. If death was not the end of life, what was it? This way of thinking was beginning to drive old Buck up a tree. That is if he could still climb a trees.

"Where are you headed this time of the night?"

"I'm taking me a walk, which is something that you should be doing, Ike. I have some heavy thinking to do and the only air that allows this kind of heavy thinking is night air. There is too much pollution when the devil is working."

"I think I'll walk along with you in case you see a ghost or wild animal, or something that scares you. You know you are too old to run."

"You show wouldn't be any help if we did run into a mad 'coon or possum. You are in worse shape than I am. Just look at ya. You can't come out of doors without that walking pole of yours."

"What's on your mind professor? I know there is something cooking in that nappy head of yours."

"Ike, I'm at a cross-road when it comes to what to believe that man's reasons are for being born. Why is the world what it is and what drives it?"

"I can't help you much in that area of your confusion. You have been acting funny for a long time. We once thought we might have to have you committed to a nut house."

"Anyway, I have come to a big conclusion about man and

his many gods. You know that I have a room full of books from every part of the world telling their stories about who they take god to be and what he, or, it is to them. Not one comes close to explaining the nature of this universe to any satisfactory level. It takes an idiot to really accept any one of these explanations for the truth."

"You have searched long enough to have answers to any question that you can ask of anybody. You are too religious Buck. You believe that there is a one-god ruler more than the rest of us. That has always been your problem."

"I'm beginning to think that you are right. I believe so much in there being some kind of power behind everything that exist until I come off seeming to believe in nothing."

Buck's community of old timers had shrunk to nearly zero. The younger generations didn't pay the old boys much attention. The young folks didn't put too much confidence in what the old people said or did. Buck had gotten his fill of reading the religious books and pamphlets about who's gods were the real gods. There didn't appear to be enough evidence or confirmation to base a devoted life on. The man thought that it was passed the time when he had a long time to think about anything.

Buck thought he would turn in early and try to get a good night's sleep for a change. He put off his usual night's walking until he did some heavy dreaming about where he should plan to go from where he was. He had a hunch where he was but had no clear idea of where he should be headed.

CHAPTER TWENTY-FOUR

THE LIGHT COMES ON

"Well, Mr. Smith, let's have a seat and talk about what we have here. I'll go over these results of these tests and explain what these answers mean."

"I pray that the results is something that I'll be able to live with. Let's get on with it, Doc."

"You have a tumor about the size of a medium size hen egg on your lung. It does have some malignancy. Just hold on here for a minute. Let's see what this says. The malignancy has not spread too much. It appears to be of the slow moving kind. Are you with me thus far, Mr. Smith? I hate telling my patients this kind of news."

"What do you have in mind that we should do about this knot on my lungs?"

"Right now, I suggest that you do absolutely nothing. Like I said, it is slow moving right now and won't be a threat to your health for a while. At your age any surgery will be risky. If you have a condition like what you have it makes more sense to let something else cause your crossing over other than an unnecessary operation."

Buck had himself something to pray about after the

conversation with his old worn out medical fake healer. His regular physician will have to have his say. But, Buck had a few questions to ask of his family doctor. He was not too surprised to hear that there was something in his insides that would sign his death warrant. There are still things about man's existence that he wanted to hear from somebody who had held hands with eternity and experienced of witnessing the end of many lives.

Buck slept on it for a few days before his appointment with his doctor came around. He made sure he had a list of the questions that he wanted his doctor's opinions on.

"Mr. Smith! Come on in and have a seat right there and I'll be with you in a minute."

"Now Mr. Smith. I see that you have a small tumor on your lungs. It does not look like it's life threatening at this time. So, having said that, what is on your mind other than the tumor?"

"Ain't that enough, Doctor? These other little ailment from old age can wait. There ain't much you can do about them anyway. Now, I want to know if there is a possible cure for something like this outside of surgery. I would like your opinion about the effects of our medical cures for such. Have you ever known people to have miracles that cured these death sentences.? Go ahead and talk to me Doctor."

"Yes, I have witnessed many so-called miracles solving problems resulting from physical ailments, and even problems that aren't physical sicknesses. These events happen all the time. They are the results of misdiagnoses, strong resistances and the powers of prayers."

"Hold it right there Doctor. The powers of prayers? Could you go a bit further and tell me how often this kind of miracles happens. The powers of prayers?"

"Yeah, I know what you may be thinking. It was hard for me to believe praying could have the powers it has. Yes, it took me years to accept that it was a fact. I've had all the evidence one needed to know for sure that what I arrived at was wrong."

"It sounds to me like prayers might offer the best cure. It sounds like the safest if one has the time."

"You have a point there about having the time. Take your case for an example, you have time to try less drastic measures than going under knife for major surgeries."

"I thank God for that. Well, I guess I'll see you later."

"I would like to schedule your appointments for every three months. That way, I'll be able to keep an eye on the tumor's growth. We don't want it to get out of hand."

Buck continued to have second thoughts about the miracle thing. It didn't make earthly sense. How could a serious ailment heal itself?

"How did your test turn out, Buck?"

"Not too good, Ike. It looks like the chickens have come home to roost. I have a cancerous tumor on my right lung. It's the size of a medium size hen egg."

"Oh my god! I'm so sorry to hear that."

"Hey, hold up here. I'm not finished telling you the rest of it. I'm not dead yet, so don't give me that goodbye look."

"Okay, go on with what you and your doctor have come up with."

"This tumor is about the size of a small egg and slow spreading. The doctor thinks I have plenty of time to decide what will be what. I know he thinks that at my age major surgery might finish me off and he won't get paid."

"He is right so far. Go on!"

"I asked him to give me some history about something that has been on my mind for a long time. I wanted to know what his experiences relative to miracles were. Did he run across any and if he did, what was his understanding of such."

"In his line of work losing patients shouldn't bother him too much. He is no stranger to the dead. Most of his patients are nearly dead anyway by the time they get to his office."

"You know what the boy said? He said that he had been an

on-the-spot witness to some miracles that even he could not come close to explaining. He told me those kinds of cures came from the hands of God. He had no other explanation. Can you believe a heart specialist believing such non-sense?"

"Yeah, I've heard them kinds of tales all my life, and so have you."

Buck and Ike made their usual stop when they had good news, bad news or no news at all. They had an excuse to take a few swigs of their favorite beverage.

Buck put all his plans for his future, his recollections of the past and his present concerns together in his mind, toward finding a solution to his tumor. He had read enough about what was credited to miracles to test a few of his own summations of his understanding of it. He decided to give his inner soul a chance to work and provide the miracles, or give some answers to man's most asked questions. He decided to have a long talk with his pastor before he decided what his complete plans were to be. He wanted to know where this god, who controlled the universe, resides at. How did mam make contact with the ruler of all things.

"Come on in Buck and drag up a chair. I hope you don't mind me inviting several of our church members to sit in on our discussion. I believe this is one of the most important discussions man can have with anybody or anything."

"I don't mind at all. The more answers I can get, the better."

"You want to know what the God of the universe is and where can he be found. Is that something like what you are concerned about?"

"Yes, something like that. I know you have gone to divinity schools all your life and have sat by the bedsides of the dying and have seem what pass for miracles take place right before your eyes. I want to hear what you make of your experiences. How have you experienced these so-called miracles?"

"Well Buck, you asked for it and here it comes. I don't believe

God will stand to be judged by man. I think you have to accept the words of the good book without questions. Man is not wise enough to question God's works. Buck, I think I understand how you feel but you will have to take God at his word."

By the time Buck got a chance to get away from the faithfuls he was in worse shape mentally than he was back in the day. He did learn a valuable lesion and that was, he had to find his God on his own. He knew that each man had to be whatever he became on his own. The troubled man went home to ponder what was his place and purpose in the world.

After several trips back to the respiratory specialist he began to get the notion that something strange was going on. The tumor seemed to be shrinking instead of growing. He knew he had decided to turn the entire project over to his inner mind and let go. He had stopped praying to the god in the sky and prayed to the god within himself. The fears that he once carried around had gone into hiding and left his insides free to function as it was created to. Buck became a new man. He was contented for the first time in his life. He felt complete.

"What happened to you Mr. Smith? I can barely detect any signs that there ever was a tumor on your right lung. What have you been doing?"

"Doctor, I thought about miracles and where they came from. I arrived at only one conclusion and that was they had to come from within the people. That told me something that I have been missing all my life."

"What was that Mr. Smith?"

"I had been looking for the answers in the wrong places, I had searched the outside world instead of searching my inner world. I now know where God lives. Every creations on earth is its own god. You, me and all others are our own god and through that god we will fulfill our mission on earth. I am my own God. Amend.

Printed in the United States
By Bookmasters